Denny Lorenz

Development of a Standard Report for Signal Verification on Public Adverse Event Databases

SCHRIFTENREIHE MASTERSTUDIENGANG CONSUMER HEALTH CARE

herausgegeben von Prof. Dr. Marion Schaefer

ISSN 1869-6627

4   *Elizabeth Storz*
    Psychopharmakamarkt in Deutschland
    Eine Untersuchung zu den Strukturveränderungen
    durch das Arzneiversorgungs-Wirtschaftlichkeitsgesetz (AVWG)
    ISBN 978-3-8382-0109-2

5   *Ursula Sellerberg*
    Heilpflanzen-Datenbanken im Internet
    Eine kritische Untersuchung anhand verbraucherrelevanter Kriterien
    ISBN 978-3-8382-0092-7

6   *Rüdiger Kolbeck*
    Arzneimittelfälschungen auf globaler und nationaler Ebene
    Eine Studie über das Problembewusstsein bei Patienten und Experten
    ISBN 978-3-8382-0155-9

7   *Silke Lauterbach*
    Das diabetische Fußsyndrom
    Ein Ratgeber zur Identifizierung von Risikopatienten in der Apotheke
    ISBN 978-3-8382-0182-5

8   *Judith Rommerskirchen*
    Die Arzneimittelrabattverträge der gesetzlichen Krankenversicherungen
    Eine Studie über Probleme bei ihrer Umsetzung an der Schnittstelle von Arzt und Apotheker
    ISBN 978-3-8382-0253-2

9   *Verena Purrucker*
    Möglichkeiten und Grenzen von Franchisesystemen in der zahnärztlichen Versorgung in Deutschland
    ISBN 978-3-8382-0186-3

10 *Stefan Prüller*
    Risiken und Nebenwirkungen auf der Spur
    Konsumentenberichte über unerwünschte Arzneimittelwirkungen als Chance für Krankenkassen
    ISBN 978-3-8382-0318-8

11 *Denny Lorenz*
    Development of a Standard Report for Signal Verification on Public Adverse Event Databases
    ISBN 978-3-8382-0432-1

Denny Lorenz

DEVELOPMENT OF A STANDARD REPORT FOR SIGNAL VERIFICATION ON PUBLIC ADVERSE EVENT DATABASES

ibidem-Verlag
Stuttgart

Bibliografische Information der Deutschen Nationalbibliothek
Die Deutsche Nationalbibliothek verzeichnet diese Publikation in der
Deutschen Nationalbibliografie; detaillierte bibliografische Daten sind im
Internet über http://dnb.d-nb.de abrufbar.

Bibliographic information published by the Deutsche Nationalbibliothek
Die Deutsche Nationalbibliothek lists this publication in the Deutsche Nationalbibliografie;
detailed bibliographic data are available in the Internet at http://dnb.d-nb.de.

∞

Gedruckt auf alterungsbeständigem, säurefreien Papier
Printed on acid-free paper

ISSN: 1869-6627

ISBN-13: 978-3-8382-0432-1

© *ibidem*-Verlag
Stuttgart 2012

Alle Rechte vorbehalten

Das Werk einschließlich aller seiner Teile ist urheberrechtlich geschützt. Jede Verwertung außerhalb der engen Grenzen des Urheberrechtsgesetzes ist ohne Zustimmung des Verlages unzulässig und strafbar. Dies gilt insbesondere für Vervielfältigungen, Übersetzungen, Mikroverfilmungen und elektronische Speicherformen sowie die Einspeicherung und Verarbeitung in elektronischen Systemen.

All rights reserved. No part of this publication may be reproduced, stored in or introduced into a retrieval system, or transmitted, in any form, or by any means (electronical, mechanical, photocopying, recording or otherwise) without the prior written permission of the publisher. Any person who does any unauthorized act in relation to this publication may be liable to criminal prosecution and civil claims for damages.

Printed in Germany

Abstract

Publically available external databases that contain adverse drug reactions, such as the FDA AERS and VigiBase database are currently not obligatorily reviewed by the pharmaceutical product manufacturers regarding potential drug safety signals. On the other hand the value of information on adverse events that is concealed here is well acknowledged by the product experts. As meanwhile appropriate tools are available that support the commonly used statistical methods of signal detection, these external data sources are now evaluated for their suitability to at least support signal verification for signals which have been detected within the company.

This study evaluates the benefit of the reports that the market leading software 'Empirica Signal' generates for common questions that are raised during the signal verification process. It will discuss, if the questions that the medical reviewers have can be appropriately addressed and if the results are able to improve the knowledge on a safety signal to ultimately help in the decision to refute or strengthen the medical or purely statistical hypothesis. In order to achieve this, the major external databases have been described and structurally assessed. All available reports from these sources have been created and analyzed using the drug event combination Sorafenib and Intestinal perforation in order to propose a standard set of reports. The applied statistical methods are discussed, as the report interpretation has to be put into their light. As a result, a standard set of the most relevant reports was developed which will now be used as a first step when reviewing a signal on external databases. It is explicitly not excluding the option to perform any further query on theses sources which addresses a specific medical question for unique signals that presumably will arise once this process is established.

Besides the selection of reports, contrary opinions on the hierarchy levels of drug and event on which the statistical scores are calculated are expected. The decision on these levels and the depths of the external analyses itself has shown to be a trade-off between scientific ambitions and the effort that is accepted to be made in a legally regulated environment. The balanced proposal however should be implemented to start using the available information and increase patient safety by more information based decisions. Experience with these reports and enhancements on the processes and tools will subsequently lead to an even wider use of the data or the determination to use sources like electronic health records to support the medical experts in pharmacovigilance with the best available data.

Öffentlich zugängliche externe Datenbanken (wie z.B. FDA AERS und VigiBase), welche unerwartete Arzneimittelwirkungen enthalten, sind aktuell kein verpflichtender Bestandteil routinemäßiger Überprüfungen von Arzneimittelherstellern im Rahmen der Signalerkennung. Andererseits ist der enorme Wert, der in solchen Datenbanken enthaltenen Informationen zu bestimmten Nebenwirkungen in der Pharmakovigilanz durchaus bekannt. Durch die Verfügbarkeit entsprechender Software, welche die gängigen statistischen Methoden der Signalerkennung beherrscht, sollen diese Informationsquellen künftig zum Zwecke der Bewertung solcher Meldungen herangezogen werden, die auf der firmeninternen Datenbank auffällig geworden sind.

Die vorliegende Studie bewertet den Nutzen der Berichte, die durch die marktführende Software ‚Empirica Signal' bezüglich der im Rahmen der Signalbewertung üblichen Fragestellungen generiert werden können. Es wird geprüft, ob solche Fragen adäquat adressierbar sind und ob die Ergebnisse potentiell einen Informationsgewinn bzgl. des untersuchten Signals darstellen, um letztendlich in der Entscheidung über die Weiterverfolgung des Signals zu helfen. Dies gilt insbesondere, wenn das Signal rein statistischer Natur ist. Die wichtigsten statistischen Methoden und Datenbanken wurden zum Zwecke der vorliegenden Studie beschrieben und ihre Struktur analysiert. Alle verfügbaren Berichte unter Verwendung der externen Quellen wurden mit der beispielhaften Nebenwirkung Darmperforationen unter Sorafenib erstellt und bewertet, um ein Standardpaket von Tabellen und Darstellungen für die allgemeine Signalbewertung vorschlagen zu können. Dieses Resultat kann nun zu Beginn einer jeden externen Signalanalyse Verwendung finden, was explizit der weiteren Nachverfolgung spezifischer medizinischer Fragestellungen für einzelne Signale nicht entgegensteht.

Neben der Auswahl der Standardberichte werden auch die verwendeten hierarchischen Ebenen von Produkt und Ereignis, die für die statistischen Berechnungen herangezogen werden, kritisch diskutiert. Es wurde gezeigt, dass die Entscheidung hierüber, sowie über die Tiefe der Analysen selbst, ein Kompromiss aus wissenschaftlichen Zielstellungen und dem in diesem gesetzlich regulierten Umfeld vertretbarem Aufwand ist. Der ausgewogene Vorschlag sollte jedoch implementiert werden, um die vorhandenen Information sinnvoll für Entscheidungen im Sinne der Patientensicherheit nutzen zu können. Die gesammelten Erfahrungen werden hilfreich sein, um jetzt und in Zukunft die Prozesse und Methoden zu verbessern, die vorhandenen Daten voll nutzen und auch auf andere Quellen übertragen zu können um die in der Pharmakovigilanz arbeitenden medizinischen Fachkräfte mit bestmöglichen Daten und Informationen zu versorgen.

List of Abbreviations

2D / 3D	Two / Three Dimensional
AE	Adverse Event
AERS	Adverse Event Reporting System
ADR	Adverse Drug Reaction
ATC	Anatomical Therapeutic Chemical
BRIC	Brazil, Russia, India, China
CCDS	Company Core Data Sheet
CI	credible interval / confidence interval
CIOMS	Council for International Organizations of Medical Sciences
DEC	Drug Event Combination
DMA	Data Mining Algorithm
DME	Designated Medical Event
EB05	lower bound of the 90% credible interval
EBGM	Empirical Bayes Geometric Mean
EEA	European Economic Area
EMA	European Medicines Agency
EVDAS	EudraVigilance Data warehouse Analysis System
FDA	Food and Drug Administration (United States of America)
HLGT	High-Level Group Term
HLT	High-Level Term
ICH	International Conference on Harmonisation
ICSR	Individual case safety report
IDRAC	International Drug Regulatory Affairs Compendium
INTSS	Interaction Signal Score
LLT	Lower Level Term
MedDRA	Medical Dictionary for Regulatory Activities
MGPS	Multi-item Gamma Poison Shrinker

MHRA	(British) Medicines and Healthcare products Regulatory Agency
NEC	not elsewhere classified
MSSO	Maintenance and Support Services Organization
OMOP	Observational Medical Outcomes Partnership
PROTECT	Pharmacoepidemiological Research on Outcomes of Therapeutics by a European Consortium
PRR	Proportional Reporting Ratio
PSUR	Periodic Safety Update Report
PT	Preferred Term
ROR	Reported Odds Ratio
RR / RRR	Relative Reporting Ratio
SDR	Signal of Disproportionate Reporting
SMQ	Standard MedDRA Query
SOC	System Organ Class
SOP	Standard Operating Procedure
SRS	Spontaneous Reporting System
WHO	World Health Organization
WP	Working Procedure
WP3	Work Package 3
VAERS	Vaccine Adverse Events Reporting System

Table of Contents

LIST OF ABBREVIATIONS	1
1. INTRODUCTION	5
2. SCOPE AND PROBLEM DEFINITION	6
3. SIGNAL DETECTION AND INVESTIGATION METHODS	9
3.1. Definition of Terms	9
3.1.1. A Drug Safety Signal	9
3.1.2. External Databases	10
3.2. Qualitative Signal Detection	10
3.3. Quantitative Signal Detection	12
3.3.1 Proportional Reporting Ratio (PRR)	14
3.3.2 Empirical Bayes Geometric Mean (EBGM)	16
3.3.3 Case Scoring Algorithms	17
4. USE OF PUBLIC ADVERSE EVENTS DATABASES	19
4.1. Objectives for Usage of External Data	19
4.2. Analysis of Available External Data Sources	20
4.2.1. United States Adverse Event Reporting System (AERS)	20
4.2.2. VigiBase	21
4.2.3. Comparison of FDA AERS and VigiBase	22
4.2.4. EudraVigilance	27
4.2.5. Data from other Health Authorities	27
4.2.6. Epidemiological Sources	28
4.3. Limitations of Spontaneous Adverse Event Reporting Databases	28
5. EVALUATION OF REPORTS FOR SIGNAL INVESTIGATION	31
5.1. Creation and Assessment of Reports within Empirica Signal	32
5.1.1. Introduction of the Example Drug Event Combination	32
5.1.2. Search Strategy in Structured Product and Event Data	33
5.1.3. Product Related Reports	36
5.1.4. Event Related Reports	45
5.1.5. Additional Reported Case Attributes	49
5.1.6. Three Dimensional (3D) Analysis	55

5.1.7. Comparison Overviews	60
5.2. Proposal on Standard Report Package	**63**
5.2.1. Output Preparation and Customization	63
5.2.2. Standard Outputs	64
5.3. Identified Gaps and Possible Enhancements	**66**
6. FUTURE WORK AND CONCLUSIONS	**67**
BIBLIOGRAPHIC REFERENCES	**VII**
INTERNET REFERENCES	**XIII**
ANNEXES	**XX**

1. Introduction

The spontaneous reporting of adverse reactions beyond a drug's market approval is currently the core information-generating method of international pharmacovigilance.[1] In addition, technical progress leads to a growing number of new data sources, such as electronic health record systems, administrative and insurance claims databases, and registries[2]. They were developed for a special purpose and are also evaluated with regard to their potential to gather pharmacovigilance information. However, today's methods of collection, evaluation, mining and interpretation of spontaneously reported adverse event (AE) data are well established and cannot easily be replaced by other approaches.
Pharmaceutical companies are required by law to maintain databases for the collection of such data and provide periodic updates on drug safety profiles. Additionally, reporting requirements to health authorities exist for a large subset of the available individual case reports and consequently let the central databases grow rapidly. Both, the number of voluntary direct reports from consumers or healthcare professionals to the authorities and the mandatory expedited and periodically reported adverse events from manufacturers are still increasing almost exponentially and are a sound base to search for rare adverse reactions or for those, which could not be detected in a clinical trial setting.[3]

The cumulative analysis of cases either through the review of listings (e.g. Periodic Safety Update Reports - PSURs) or through statistical methods on a company's database is required by law. Irregular occurrences or frequencies of reported AEs (potential signals) which are arising during this review have to be evaluated in detail. Statistical methods such as disproportionality algorithms rely on the background population of the database in which the signal was detected. Hence, it is useful to compare the data with the content of large public databases using a potentially more inhomogeneous set of individual case safety reports (ICSRs) to understand, if similar figures, trends or even hints to a drug class effect, confounding or other phenomena can be found.

---

[1] Lindquist M. (2008), p.417.
[2] United States Food and Drug Administration (2011), 1.
[3] European Commission (2008), p.36.

2. Scope and Problem Definition

Potential safety signals which need further evaluation can arise from various sources. There might be a series of cases that was received over time, pointing always to a similar adverse reaction. This pattern can be detected during traditional signal detection methods such as single case review. The pattern also could have been detected through more modern signal detection using statistical methods (signal of disproportionate reporting). A question from a third party (e.g. health authority) regarding a certain product and a particular adverse event might need further analysis, even if there was not one single case received by the marketing authorization holder yet. Another scenario where maybe just one well documented, convincing report was received and the causal relationship between the administered drug and the reported side-effect is evidenced by e.g. positive re-challenge (index case) can be considered a potential signal.

For the review of the company's drug safety database there are often very detailed listings or tools available that might be custom built or bought from the safety system vendor. They have access to all the very detailed single case information that was captured according to the data entry rules which the company determined. Interpretation of such standardized data is unlikely to be accidently wrong if the entry rules are followed and the quality is assured through documented measures. How to use the various internal tools for signal detection or investigation is usually documented in standard operation procedures (SOPs) or working procedures (WPs).

As of now, for external databases there is no detailed legislation available on how it should be accessed and integrated into the signal detection or verification process. Nevertheless, regulatory authorities are using their data sources for their own signal detection purposes already – gaining more and more knowledge about the underlying statistical methods and interpretation of the cumulative data and scores. They are realizing that adverse event databases, even if they exceed figures of 4 million[4] single case reports for the United States Food and Drug Administration (FDA) or even 6 million[5] for the World Health Organization (WHO) are still not sufficient to assess a pharmaceutical drug's safety profile completely. They want to access much larger sources with three digit millions of patient records in order to

---

[4] United States Food and Drug Administration (2010).
[5] World Health Organization (2011).

scan them for signals.[6] This concludes, that even though it is not mandatory yet to perform signal detection on the available external data, a mid-size to large-size company should at least use these sources to gain additional knowledge about a particular potential signal to be proactive in the field of their authorized products in respect to signal detection. If this is not done, there is a certain risk that the expertise on public AE data and closely related other health data stays with the competent authorities and safety signals might be detected by them rather than by the company itself.

When starting to look into the external AE data sources for a potential signal regarding a specific drug event combination (DEC) there are basically two general options on how to proceed with the exploration. The first one is to decide on the requested listings, scores, graphs and figures based on the nature of the product or event under evaluation. The second option would be to always provide a standard set of such reports.

Whereas both options do not exclude each other it seems to be more meaningful to choose the first one because every safety signal could be unique and needs a unique set of analyses. On the other hand, this would include a very detailed and medically validated investigation planning upfront for each DEC which is evaluated on external data. This is a resource intensive task which could be avoided by providing a standard set of reports first to see if any question remains unanswered. If so, additional reports could be requested in a second step with additional knowledge on what detailed question should be penetrated exactly. Additionally, the availability of a standard package of data analysis might be valuable in situations, where there are different medical opinions on what data could exactly be helpful for a particular DEC.

It was acknowledged by the Council for International Organizations of Medical Sciences (CIOMS) VIII working group, that even though stepwise investigation of safety data with its very flexible approaches is an integral part of pharmacovigilance, the use of consistent methods and processes is critical to obtain "a consistent approach across all sources of safety data".[7] A standard set of reports will ensure that during signal investigation the initial steps are process-wise harmonized and comparable. It will also invalidate proactively the subliminal presumption that data analysis and assessment activities would attempt to focus on 'good' results.

---

[6] Rosati (2009), p. 173.
[7] CIOMS Working Group VIII (2010), p. 92.

The following chapters will discuss the common safety signal detection and investigation methods on spontaneous AE databases to understand their nature and give guidance on the interpretation of signal scores by analyzing which type or presentation of data is helpful for a product expert. Information on publicly available databases will be gathered to determine if there is a benefit in using one or the other data source in a given situation. It will be analyzed which reports, graphs and figures can be pulled from the external data using a software which is used by pharmaceutical companies as well as health authorities. These outputs will be put in the light of the previously collected information to determine what the content of a standard set for a signal investigation on an external database should cover.

3. Signal Detection and Investigation Methods

3.1. Definition of Terms

3.1.1. A Drug Safety Signal

Several definitions exist for what is considered to be a drug safety signal. The WHO defines a signal as information from usually more than one single case "on a possible causal relationship between an adverse event and a drug, the relationship being previously unknown or incompletely documented".[8] The FDA considers every "excess of adverse events compared to what would be expected to be associated with a product's use" a signal.[9] Also broader definitions can be found where signalling is to be understood as the "detection of early warning signs" and a signal is a set of (usually clinical, pharmacological, pathological or epidemiological) data "constituting a hypothesis that is relevant to the rational and safe use of a medicine".[10]

As signal detection is an important part of pharmacovigilance, the term 'safety signal' has to be used carefully. Ideally, it should be placed into suitable context as precise and informative as possible[11] and not without further elaboration to avoid misinterpretation. The term 'signal' is best used for a DEC which has undergone some clinical judgement[12] (clinical signal) in contrast to a purely "statistical or quantitative signal"[13] or signal of disproportionate reporting (SDR). SDRs however always need to be further evaluated to strengthen and to confirm, respectively, or to refute them.

According to the CIOMS VIII working group another term in the same context that can be used is the 'potential risk' which is a risk attributable to the drug (e.g. associated reaction for other products of the same class) but without being supported by human evidence (e.g. an adverse event reported).[14] This study will use the FDA's signal definition as mainly statistical signals will be explored.

---

[8] World Health Organization (2002), p. 6.
[9] United States Food and Drug Administration (2005), p.4.
[10] Meyboom et al. (1997), p.355
[11] Manfred Hauben, Lester Reich (2005), p.480.
[12] ibid.
[13] CIOMS Working Group XIII (2010), p. 14.
[14] CIOMS Working Group VIII (2010), p. 14.

3.1.2. External Databases

In the following chapters the term 'External Database' will be used for all electronic data storage systems which are generated and used for different purposes outside the responsibility of a pharmaceutical company and contain information, which potentially would allow to investigate a certain drug safety question. These external databases are considered to be a 'Public Database' if it is publicly available due to national legislations but they might also be only accessible after purchasing a license for its use. A database in which the raw data is not available for further investigation but results from detailed analysis on the existing data are published (either to the public or to the marketing authorization holders) does not fulfil the criteria for a public database.

The main difference to an internal or 'in-house' database is, that the available datasets are collected from various sources and are not harmonized in terms of data entry conventions. There might be for example a mixture of different conventions regarding the coding of reported terms using the Medical Dictionary for Regulatory Activities (MedDRA). In a company's database the marketing authorization holder has full control over keeping the data consistent.

3.2. Qualitative Signal Detection

If there is no automated support on analyzing individual case reports on suspected adverse events, the only way to detect potential signals is to have each of these reports reviewed by an experienced assessor or by a team of experts. The qualitative signal detection is performed as the assessment of the likelihood, that the clinical picture has been caused by the drug and is a purely intellectual method based on a case-by-case analysis.[15] This manual procedure is also referred to as traditional signal detection.[16]

One single individual report will only be considered a signal as an exception, usually in cases of very severe adverse events. It has to be well documented and has to meet certain requirements (e.g. re-challenge) that justifies to classify the report as an index-case.[17] How many cases are needed to provide sufficient evidence for a signal differs and depends on the quality and source of the cases but also on the nature of the adverse events itself and whether there is a possible pharmacological rationale available to explain them.

---

[15] Egberts (2007), p. 607-608.
[16] van Manen, Fram, DuMouchel (2007), p. 453.
[17] Meyboom et al. (1997), p.361.

While a medical review is certainly valuable it is at the same time very time-consuming and might not be efficient considering today's amount of reported adverse events. A high number of reports that are evaluated by a single person, even if well trained, might limit the possibility to detect trends in reporting or to identify relationships between case attributes like dosing information or patient demographics. Other potential problems concerning repeatability and consistency between different medicinal experts and continuity after staff leave also need to be considered in pharmaceutical companies.

Therefore, it is acknowledged that the traditional methods of data gathering and evaluation cannot be replaced by data mining alone as they are the "cornerstone of pharmacovigilance activities"[18]. Pharmaceutical companies design their pharmacovigilance processes still in a way that relevant cases are reviewed by medical experts. In that sense, the quantitative signal detection which will be described later is a way to prioritize this labour intensive work. Regulatory authorities demand a manual review at the moment indirectly through the request to provide Periodic Safety Update Reports (PSURs)[19] which list adverse events but also provide figures on patient exposure with a product or active substance. The general exposure of the public is often only determined by surrogate values as for example sales figures as the so called 'under-reporting' of adverse events is a known fact. Still, it is at least possible to be able to see trends or changes in frequencies with these approximate numbers. As an example a certain reaction which was reported five times as often as in the previous PSUR period without the suspected drug being sold more often or without any other obvious explanation will certainly be noticed by the author of the report or the reviewing body.

Qualitative signals for a product can also arise from other sources. There might be already identified risks existing which are documented e.g. in a Risk Management Plan. Such risks can be adverse drug reactions that are associated to other drugs of the same class but have not been discovered in clinical trials. They need to be systematically evaluated as soon as the product is placed on the market. The chance that such reactions still could occur after the launch is often considered high[20]. Usually, these risks are further explored in post-marketing studies but also the spontaneous reporting of such events can be put under a special monitoring process. The responsible medical product expert should be alerted in any instance.

---

[18] CIOMS Working Group VIII (2010), p.9.
[19] German Federal Institute for Drugs and Medical Devices, Medicines Act, §63b (5).
[20] European Commission (2008), p.44.

With such alerts the first occurrence of a monitored AE will be recognized immediately and a qualitative signal investigation can be initiated. Similarly, comparable or related product compounds or substances are reviewed for adverse drug reaction (ADR) or AE reports in the literature. This may or may not lead to a signal but further investigation needs to take place in any case. One of two more generic concepts is to classify certain events as medically important to expose them to a more detailed or skilled review.[21] The other considers Designated Medical Events (DMEs) - reactions that are often drug related, inherently serious and consequently qualify for a high-priority review when analyzing a drug safety profile especially of new molecular entities.[22]

The following are typical examples of DMEs[23]:

- Aplastic anaemia;
- Severe skin reactions, e.g. toxic epidermal necrolysis, Stevens-Johnson syndrome;
- Torsade de pointes; and
- Hepatic failure.

Third party requests from health authorities, license partners or health organizations such as the WHO, regarding a certain product's attributable risk are also further investigated. Traditionally, this is done on the company's drug safety database, in the existing clinical trial data or again through literature review. The number of such requests will most likely increase and the percentage of reasons for the request will necessarily move partially from more general medical judgment and concerns to suspiciously high reporting ratios for unexpected events.[24,25] To understand the latter type, the medical expert will gain additional information if he or she has access to the same data as the requester in this scenario.

3.3. Quantitative Signal Detection

The traditional qualitative signal detection approaches alone may be sufficient in situations where a company has only a limited product portfolio and the spontaneous reporting database contains a low number of adverse event reports. Inde-

---

[21] European Medicines Agency (2011).
[22] United States Food and Drug Administration (2008), 1, p.3.
[23] CIOMS Working Group VIII (2010), p.42.
[24] European Medicines Agency (2010).
[25] United States Federal Business Opportunities (2010).

pendent from the fact that the purchasing and implementation costs of signal detection software plus its maintenance and validation might not be affordable for a smaller company, the statistical methods that are usually applied might not even work as desired in a small heterogeneous database. These statistical methods, also often referred to as data mining algorithms (DMAs) have been developed for target databases that contain a relatively large dataset of adverse events reported spontaneously across a variety of medicinal products. The methods that are in use today mainly analyze the disproportionality of reporting for a certain DEC against the same event reported for other drugs (background dataset). They aim not to replace the traditional approaches but rather to structure a large volume of data into smaller fractions of certain interest to help in mitigating the risk of detecting issues too late.

Automated approaches to signal detection may still be seen as not fully established since there is no regulation that mandates such methods to marketing authorization holders at the moment. However, these computer-aided methodologies have already a history starting close to when modern medicinal product laws were established. Already at that time they considered parameters, such as number of reports, source and types of reports, seriousness of the reaction, number of deaths, rechallenges, rate of reporting, when the drug was released, and similar reactions in a related drug as important.[26] The commonly known proportional reporting ratio (PRR) was first published in 1974 and publications using this and related algorithms can be found since the middle of the 1990s.[27]

---

[26] Napke (1968), p. 68.
[27] CIOMS Working Group VIII (2010), p.49.

3.3.1 Proportional Reporting Ratio (PRR)

The PRR is one very commonly used method to calculate the disproportionality of a reported DEC. In general, disproportionality algorithms compare expected values with what was observed in reality. It is using pre-defined thresholds to determine whether a deviation from the expected number of reports is unexpected or irregular and should therefore be reviewed.

For the basic calculation a 2x2 contingency table is used which divides all available reports into four quadrants depending on if the suspected drug was given or not and whether the ADR occurred or not.

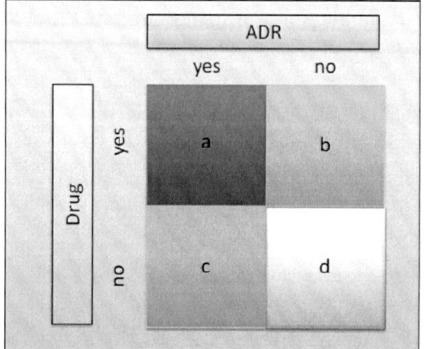

Figure 1:   Basic contingency table.
Source: Own presentation following CIOMS working group VIII (2010), p.53.

The disproportionality is the ratio of the number of observed divided by the number of expected reports. If the number of expected reports is the average occurrence independent of any given drug then this translates into the concept of the 'Relative Reporting Ratio' (RR or RRR) and is calculated using the following formula[28]:

$$RR = \frac{a}{a+b} \bigg/ \frac{a+c}{a+b+c+d} = \frac{a}{\frac{(a+b)(a+c)}{a+b+c+d}}$$

---

[28] Begaud (2000), p.30.

The following picture shows a simplified distribution of these reports in a database.

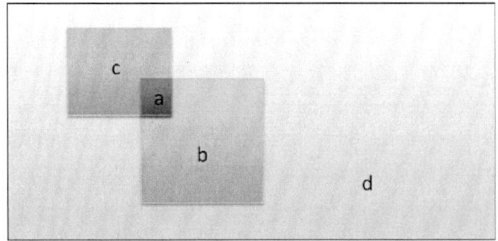

Figure 2: Simplified case distribution in an adverse events database.
Source: Own presentation.

The RR calculation considers the available cases with the DEC (a) which occurred with the drug (a and b) for the calculation of the expected amount of reports. The difference in the PRR calculation is basically, that these reports (a and b) are excluded from the calculation of the expected reports. This adds complexity to the calculation but is easier to be interpreted especially if ICSRs with the drug make a high percentage of the overall database. The PRR is calculated as follows[29]:

$$PRR = \frac{a}{a+b} \bigg/ \frac{c}{c+d} = \frac{a}{\frac{(a+b)c}{c+d}}$$

Any PRR value which is greater than 1 exceeds the expectation. An event which has a smaller PRR value can be explained by chance, which means, that the particular AE is not occurring more often with this drug than with any other drug. If the PRR has for example a value of 2 this means, that the vent was reported twice as often together with the drug under investigation as with any other drug in the database. To strengthen the statistical association, usually thresholds are applied when calculating disproportionality which combines two or more elements of information. They are listed below with the usually applied thresholds in brackets.[30]

- The PRR itself (≥ 2)
- The value of the Chi-square test (≥ 4)
- The total number of reports (≥ 3)

---

[29] Evans, Waller, Davis (2001), p.484.
[30] ibid.

- The lower bound of the 95% confidence interval (CI) for the PRR (≥ 1)

3.3.2 Empirical Bayes Geometric Mean (EBGM)

A low number of reports has a strong impact on the PRR score. To address this problem, shrinkage of the relative reporting ratio towards one can be done using a Bayesian framework to determine the empirical Bayes geometric mean estimate.[31]

The EBGM scores are calculated by determining the RR and applying the so called multi-item gamma poison shrinker (MGPS) model. The lower bound of the 90% credible interval of the EBGM is used to determine statistical significance. This value is referred to as EB05 and is used by regulatory authorities such as the British Medicines and Healthcare products Regulatory Agency (MHRA). As with the PRR usually more than one information component is defined as a threshold (MHRA thresholds[32] in brackets) when reviewing potential signals:

- the EBGM score itself (≥ 2.5),
- the total number of reports (≥ 3) and
- the lower bound of the credible interval, EB05 (≥ 1.8).

The following chart displays the development of the PRR versus the EBGM score for Varenicline & Abnormal Dreams over time starting with a low number of reports.

---

[31] Bate, Evans (2009), p.429.
[32] Medicines and Healthcare products Regulatory Agency (2010), p.15.

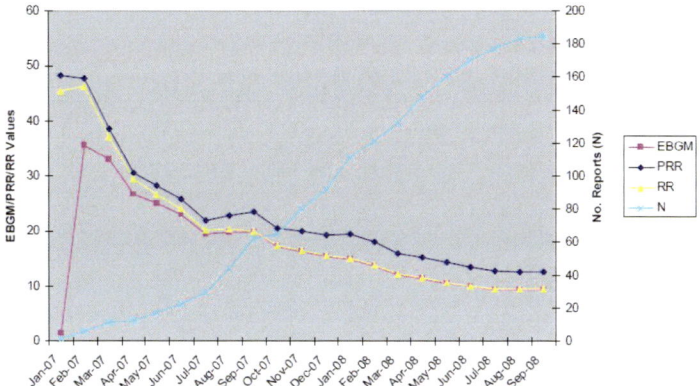

Figure 3: EBGM vs PRR for Varenicline & Abnormal Dreams (on the MHRA database)
Source: Medicines and Healthcare products Regulatory Agency (2010), p.16.

3.3.3 Case Scoring Algorithms

A frequently expressed concern on statistical methods considering disproportionate reporting for the detection of adverse drug reactions is that there can be a single case that is already sufficient to become a confirmed signal and lead to a change in the product labelling or other related decisions. With the thresholds applied in the previous chapters this concern is valid since a minimum of three cases is usually required to automatically flag a DEC.

To overcome this limitation case scoring algorithms can be implemented in parallel. These algorithms are calculating a numeric score for every case in the database considering case attributes as for example seriousness criteria, the causality assessments and the completeness of documentation. All possible values in the database are multiplied with a weighting factor and are then added up to a final case score. The scores are then again summarized when there are multiple cases with the same reported drug event combination. The later is important to detect clusters of cases even if a causal relationship was not assigned to the single case.

Similar to the signal scores of disproportionate reporting, thresholds can be applied and the case scores can be used to prioritize the work of the medical reviewers. Stop lists of known events or confounding DECs can be used in addition to avoid known or already evaluated side-effects being found at the top all the time.

4. Use of Public Adverse Events Databases

4.1. Objectives for Usage of External Data

As described before, external databases can be used for detection and verification of drug safety signals. Usually pharmaceutical companies are cautious about this topic because any new information that comes to the attention of an employee needs to be carefully evaluated regarding the potential actions that are subsequently required by law. Especially, if the interpretation of data or calculated statistical values is already difficult for an expert on that topic, an uninformed view on the same data is dangerous. In order to protect an organization from that danger a management approval for such activities can help to keep the responsible persons informed. As a negative example the data could be used to evaluate the risk profile of the drug against a competitor drug and incorrect assumptions could be drawn from the data and used for marketing purposes.

Standard operating procedures can be used to define the approval process and decide in which situations external databases are used and for which purpose. If it is decided to start a review with every DEC investigation and this is made mandatory in the respective SOP then it is essential to be compliant to this process and plan for the additional resources that are needed.

This study will focus on the verification of signals where the expectation is to be able to test the signal hypothesis on external databases in order to strengthen or weaken it. The hypothesis can arise from qualitative signal detection, quantitative signal detection or even by third party requests such as from regulatory authorities. This will be achieved by reviewing reports from the software Empirica Signal which will be described later.

Beyond the signal verification the external spontaneous reporting adverse event databases have also potential for signal detection. They can, for example, be used for newly approved medicinal products where post-marketing reporting data is already available for competitor products on the public database. Potential issues that the competitor has, may be visible in signal scores when they are relatively new and not yet published or listed since this is usually a time consuming process.

4.2. Analysis of Available External Data Sources

4.2.1. United States Adverse Event Reporting System (AERS)

The FDA is collecting all post-authorization ICSRs in the AERS database since 1997.[33] AE reporting is mandatory for drug manufacturers but also voluntary reports from healthcare professionals (such as e.g. physicians, pharmacists and nurses) and consumers (such as patients, family members, lawyers, etc.) are accepted.[34] Adverse events that have been reported earlier, starting in 1969, were stored in the Spontaneous Reporting System (SRS) database and have been migrated to AERS. The data is partially made available following the Freedom of Information Act. Data such as patient names, healthcare professional details, hospital or geographical identifiers as well as the case narratives are withheld.[35] Information that is available covers

- demographic and administrative information,
- drug information from the case reports,
- reaction information from the reports,
- patient outcome information from the reports,
- information on the source of the reports,
- a 'README' file containing a description of the files.[36]

The FDA is releasing the information relatively late. As of May 2011 third quarter 2010 (Q3 2010) datasets were available and will be used in this study. The database contains 4.272.735 individual cases in total according to an analysis performed with Empirica Signal. The most frequently reported event in AERS is Drug ineffective (~5.6% of all cases) followed by Nausea (4.2%), Headache (3.4%), Dizziness (3.3%), Dyspnoea (3.2%), Vomiting (3.1%), Dermatitis (2.8%), Pyrexia (2.8%), Diarrhoea (2.6%) and Asthenia (2.5%) which sum up to one third of the whole database. This is important information in the context of disproportionality analysis as these examples show that there is a large percentage of cases where these events would be expected.

Besides these, perhaps considered as medically unimportant events, there are also clusters of more severe reactions such as Myocardial infarction which is the event

---

[33] CIOMS Working Group XIII (2010), p. 131.
[34] United States Food and Drug Administration (2009), 2.
[35] United States Food and Drug Administration (2011), 2.
[36] United States Food and Drug Administration (2011), 3.

in the most frequently reported DEC together with Rofecoxib (more than 17.000 reported cases). Rofecoxib also has the second highest amount of cases in total with approximately 58.000 ICSRs (leading drug is the immunosuppressant Etanercept with more than 86.000 cases). Another cluster example is breast cancer which can be found in more than 38.000 cases with Estrogens Conjugated, Medroxyprogesterone and the combination of both (number of reports in total for these drugs is 86.000).[37]

The FDA also keeps a separate adverse events reporting system for vaccines (VAERS) which is not included in the standard Empirica Signal datasets. This database contains more than 123.000 reports, collected since 1990.[38]

4.2.2. VigiBase

The WHO is operating the WHO International database VigiBase since 1968. It is collecting data from more than 100 national pharmacovigilance centers which are sending updates at least every quarter.[39] The available case information is similar to FDA AERS but not made public in general. However, the data can be accessed through various licensing and fee options.[40]

Datasets are released relatively quickly compared to AERS. In May 2011 the data from first quarter 2011 (Q1 2011) was already available in Empirica Signal for analyses and contained 6.194.443 reports.[41]

With regard to the country of origin the WHO released the below statistics on their website regarding the distribution of ICSRs in VigiBase.

---

[37] The figures described in this section was pulled from AERS (Q3 2010 data) by the author.
[38] United States Food and Drug Administration (2009), 1.
[39] World Health Organization (2011), 1.
[40] World Health Organization (2011), 2.
[41] Own analysis using Empirica Signal.

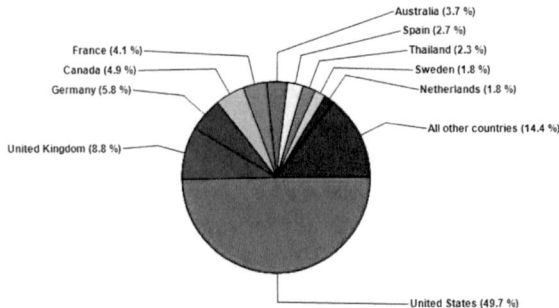

Figure 4: Distribution of ICSR per country in VigiBase as of Apr 2011.
Source: World Health Organization (2011), 1.

The distribution of cases is important information since countries with a relatively high contribution to the overall database have a strong impact on how the background population or 'noise' needs to be interpreted. With approximately 50 percent of the cases coming from the United States the corresponding reporting habits, with regards to under-reporting or media induced reporting of events, need to be considered.

4.2.3. Comparison of FDA AERS and VigiBase

Since FDA AERS and VigiBase are available in Empirica Signal this chapter will outline more differences and similarities regarding the nature of cases available in both databases.

The below figure displays the development of case counts for both databases from 1968 until the end of Q1 2011 (AERS end of Q3 2010). From the 1980's VigiBase contained more individual cases than AERS, breaking the 3 million and 4 million cases level around five years earlier. Whereas historically VigiBase is containing approximately 2 million cases more than AERS, both database volumes are increasing with almost the same speed at the moment. The drop in VigiBase's growth in the last period can be explained with the quick release of data and several cases still to arrive from national centers for this period.

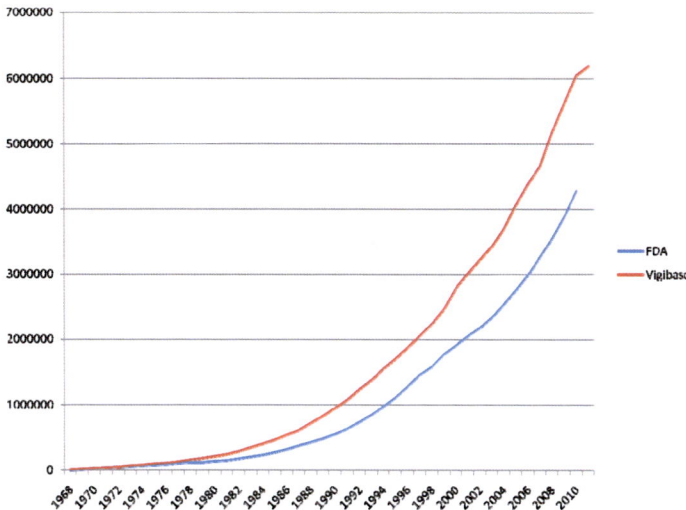

Figure 5: Growth of total case count on FDA AERS and VigiBase.
Source: Own presentation.

Knowledge about the background population with regard to reported AEs is as important as having a large dataset to reduce statistically random effects. How serious and non-serious events are handled can be different per collecting organization but also different per country. If for example a database contains only serious adverse events, it is likely that events which are usually regarded as non-serious will have high PRRs. Events which are usually serious will have lower PRRs on such a database because the background is filled with serious events. The figure below shows the distribution of serious and non-serious cases on the FDA AERS and VigiBase database.

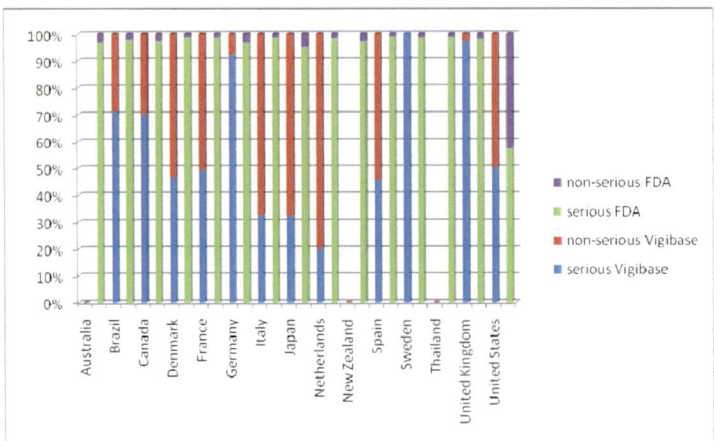

Figure 6: Percentage of non-serious vs. serious cases on FDA AERS and VigiBase per country.
Source: Own presentation.

Beyond cases from the United States the AERS database contains almost only serious cases. This is because of the FDA's reporting regulations that require marketing authorization holders to send foreign cases only when they are serious and unlabelled. AERS contains about 2.5 million serious cases from the United States (58.9% of the domestic cases)[42]. The situation in VigiBase is different. Whereas for the United States the ratio of serious and non-serious events is similar to AERS, only three of the 15 countries that exceed 1% of total cases in VigiBase or AERS report almost only serious cases (Sweden, Germany, United Kingdom). For this analysis only 2.6 million cases could be analyzed on VigiBase because the remaining cases do not carry the 'serious' attribute in Empirica Signal. As per WHO only about 10% of the cases in VigiBase are serious.[43]

The most frequently reported events in AERS have already been named. In addition to that, the figure below is displaying the distribution of events per System Organ Class (SOC) as defined in MedDRA.

---

[42] Own analysis using FDA AERS Q3 2010 data.
[43] CIOMS Working Group XIII (2010), p. 135.

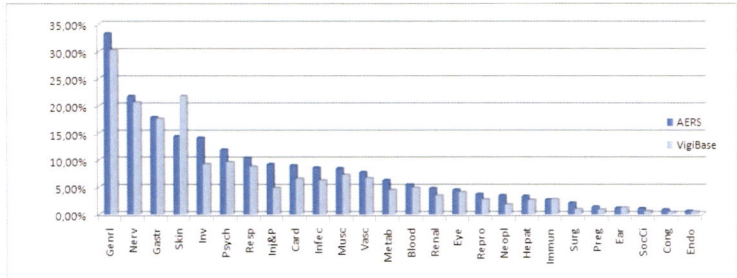

Figure 7: Distribution of events per MedDRA SOC in FDA AERS and VigiBase.
Source: Own presentation.

The figure shows that in general the distribution of events is similar between both databases. VigiBase contains proportionally more reports in the SOC Skin and subcutaneous tissue disorders than AERS. AERS stands out in the SOCs 'Injury, poisoning and procedural complications' as well as in 'Investigations' which could be explained again by the general reporting of serious compared to non-serious events.

As expected, the distribution of cases per country of incidence is dominated by domestic cases in the United States FDA AERS database. According to the data in Empirica Signal 2.6 Mio cases are without an assignment of country in AERS. 53% of these cases are serious. The figures below display the proportion of each country in the AERS and VigiBase data. Every country that contributes at least to 1% to the total cases in one of both databases was considered for display.

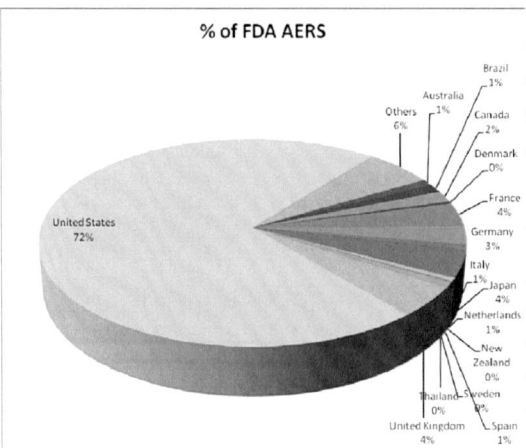

Figure 8: Country distribution in FDA AERS.
Source: Own presentation.

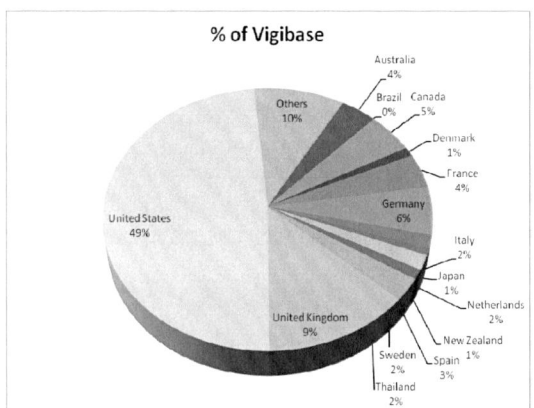

Figure 9: Country distribution in VigiBase.
Source: Own presentation.

According to this analysis about 15 countries provide 90% of all adverse events if the databases would be combined. Emerging countries such as e.g. Brazil, Russia, India and China (BRIC) are far underrepresented in AE collection, considering that these countries are home of 40% of the world's population.[44] As pharmacovigilance activities will increase in these countries the corresponding AEs will be available in AERS and VigiBase by then. The WHO's initiative in these countries will certainly increase data availability in VigiBase more than in AERS already on a short-term basis.[45]

4.2.4. EudraVigilance

The European Medicines Agency (EMA) is holding a central database for adverse event reporting in the European Economic Area (EEA). It contains more than two million cases from spontaneous sources plus more than 140.000 cases from clinical trials as of end of 2009. The cases are reported from European regulatory authorities (which mostly still own their domestic databases), marketing authorization holders and study sponsors.[46]

Currently, the data is only accessible for the EEA member states as well as for the marketing authorization holder who reported the case to EudraVigilance. With the upcoming new European legislation some of the post-authorization data will become publicly accessible. As of today there are no details available on how this will exactly work and if tools like Empirica Signal can be used for e.g. signal verification or if access to the EudraVigilance Data warehouse Analysis System (EVDAS) will be granted. As not only accessibility but also the regulations on data collection will change this is an important topic to follow with respect to signal detection and verification as in the future every spontaneously reported adverse event that occurred in the EEA will be available in EudraVigilance together with all serious cases from other countries.

4.2.5. Data from other Health Authorities

There is no single authority besides the FDA that has collected a comparable amount of adverse events. Some are also releasing data to the public and also perform signal detection on their local databases. The overview provided by the CIOMS Working Group VIII[47] can be used to find out, if individual other databases can still be used for signal verification by external users in certain scenarios (e.g. adverse events limited to one country only). In the view of the ongoing changes concerning EudraVigilance however, it is most likely that there will be an

---

[44] Investor Daily (2006).
[45] Gupta (2010), p. 21.
[46] Touraille (2010), p. 14.
[47] CIOMS Working Group VIII (2010), p.121.

American (FDA AERS), a European (EudraVigilance) and one 'any country' (VigiBase) data source for adverse event mining left after a consolidation phase.

4.2.6. Epidemiological Sources

Even though this study is focussing on spontaneous adverse event reporting databases, the current initiatives for broadening the information collection to epidemiological sources need to be described briefly.

The United States have launched the Sentinel Initiative in 2008 in order to "complement existing systems that the Agency has in place"[48] in order to allow a more evidence based evaluation of adverse drug reactions and the resulting risks. The combination of electronic health records, insurance claims and other data will increase the denominator for signal detection to more than 100 million records. Since this system is under development, it still has to prove that indeed new drug safety signals can be found utilizing information from different sources which are not comparable with regard to their internal structure and purpose. From a statistical point of view however, the additional background population can theoretically improve the sensitivity and specificity of data mining methods.[49] This will reduce false-positive and false-negative findings.

Similarly, the Observational Medical Outcomes Partnership (OMOP) is researching "methods that are feasible and useful to analyze existing healthcare databases to identify and evaluate safety and benefit issues of drugs already on the market".[50] Sub-ordinate targets are the creation of an environmental landscape which is drawn by analyzing data sources that are participating in the partnership. Also, a universal data model and terminology is developed and applied to these sources to be able to execute standardized database queries across them.

4.3. Limitations of Spontaneous Adverse Event Reporting Databases

As it relies on patients' and health care professionals' active participation, adverse event reporting databases have certain inherent limitations. The most prominent is the under-reporting since many factors can influence the reporting behaviour of an individual person.[51] Also, as described in the previous chapters, the quality and availability of data used for signal score calculations are different from ICSR to ICSR and have also changed over time with new reporting requirements. As such, adverse event reporting databases can not be used to calculate incidences but still

---

[48] United States Food and Drug Administration (2011), 1.
[49] CIOMS Working Group VIII (2010), p.102.
[50] OMOP (2011).
[51] United States Food and Drug Administration (2009), 2.

to "supply a hypothesis that should be substantiated or possibly confirmed by other methods".[52] Still, retrospective analyses of EudraVigilance reports with signal detection algorithms have shown that drug safety problems can be detected earlier than without using these methods.[53]

---

[52] CIOMS Working Group VIII (2010), p. 28.
[53] Alvarez, et al. (2010), p.487.

5. Evaluation of Reports for Signal Investigation

After a potential signal is identified there are various options to perform an analysis on publicly available external data. One option is to load the available data into a custom database for further analysis. This gives full flexibility but also bears the need to develop and validate the tools which are used for the data load and analysis as well as the potential data cleaning and standardization process. As multiple data sources are of increasing interest and new datasets are released periodically there has to be a process in place to update the data and maintain the custom architecture. If there are already tools available for performing quantitative data analysis on the company's database the data could be loaded into the same environment to minimize the effort on the implementation of data mining algorithms.

As important as the data itself and the implemented statistical methods are the documentation and tracking of signals. This process can utilize a separated system but there are good reasons for integrating the calculation of signal scores on the internal as well as on the external data ideally with the associated report production and signal tracking. An example is the deployment of code lists with regard to substances and their listed events. Once this is done, it is not only reducing workload but also minimizes the risk of classification errors. Another reason for the integration is the possibility to display counts or scores from both the internal and the external data source for a DEC in question in one report. This enables the reviewer to compare the underlying data comprehensively.

Besides a custom implementation, available commercial software can be used alternatively. This choice is releasing the efforts for implementation and maintenance that were described above. Additional benefits can be expected when choosing a software vendor who has already a long experience with the statistical methods preferably used and the data which is analyzed.

If the decision is made for a vendor with a high market share the user community (own company and other customers of the same vendor) can be used as a catalyst for getting started with the application to understand the available features and most importantly to discuss the interpretation of the results if needed. With an early and active participation there is also an option to bring in own ideas on how to implement current approaches in signal detection which the vendor can implement in future releases of his software. Compared to a custom built system it is highly likely that the total cost of ownership is lower when deciding for off-the-shelf software. Here it becomes essential to conduct a detailed vendor selection when deciding for one or the other offer. Even though there is an ongoing consolidation of pharmacovigilance software vendors and it is assumed that there will be only two left on the market soon[54], the Bayer Pharma AG considered 13 different options during the selection phase in 2009.

The company decided after considering different options for the vendor Phase Forward – which was acquired by Oracle in 2010[55] - with its product Empirica Signal. One of the main points that led to the decision was that the software is not only used by seven out of the top ten pharmaceutical companies but also by regulators like FDA and MHRA.[56] But the software is currently not used by the Bayer Pharma AG for SDR reviews mainly because of a missing evaluation of the available options. To close this gap and in order to start a systematic review as part of the standard signal verification process Empirica Signal will be used in the following chapters to produce reports for a given DEC.

5.1. Creation and Assessment of Reports within Empirica Signal

5.1.1. Introduction of the Example Drug Event Combination

The Pharmacoepidemiological Research on Outcomes of Therapeutics by a European Consortium (PROTECT) is an EMA coordinated project "that comprises a programme to address limitations of current methods in the field of pharmacoepidemiology and pharmacovigilance"[57]. Within this project the work package 3 (WP3) 'Methods for signal detection' deals with assessing and developing signal detection methods to be applied on spontaneous reports, electronic health records and clinical trial data.[58]

One of the DECs which is used for the methodology research by PROTECT WP3 is Sorafenib and the adverse event Intestinal Perforation. Sorafenib is used for the treatment of hepatocellular carcinoma. Another indication is the "treatment of patients with advanced renal cell carcinoma where an interferon-alpha or interleukin-2 based therapy has failed or who are considered unsuitable for such therapy"[59]. Sorafenib is sold under the proprietary name Nexavar by Bayer Healthcare with a total turnover of 705 million Euro in 2010.[60]

---

[54] Fitzmartin, Wise (2010), p.12.
[55] Oracle (2010), 1.
[56] Oracle (2010), 2 bottom.
[57] PROTECT (2011), 1 homepage.
[58] PROTECT (2011), 2 work programme – WP3.
[59] European Commission (2011).
[60] Bayer Pharma AG (2011).

Gastrointestinal perforation is "a hole that develops through the entire wall of the stomach, small intestine, large bowel, or gallbladder"[61] and is a medical emergency condition. This adverse reaction was found in 2006 and added to the Company Core Data Sheet (CCDS) of Sorafenib. This DEC example will be primarily used in the following chapters.

5.1.2. Search Strategy in Structured Product and Event Data

One of the main advantages using an external database is the opportunity to review characteristics and signal scores for products which are not represented in the company's adverse events database. This refers to drugs containing the same active pharmacological substance (e.g. generic products) where every manufacturer is usually only collecting and reporting the ICSRs which suspect their product and therefore owns only a subset of all cases associated with the active ingredient. Even more importantly, it also applies to products which are not identical but similar regarding their mechanism of action.

Both the FDA AERS as well as the VigiBase database drugs are coded using the WHO Anatomical Therapeutic Chemical (ATC) classification system in Empirica Signal (for the AERS data the products are ATC coded by the software vendor and not by the FDA). As the name suggests, the ATC classification groups all products "according to the organ or system on which they act and their therapeutic, pharmacological and chemical properties" using five hierarchy levels[62]:

1. anatomical main group (e.g. L: antineoplastic and immunomodulating agents)
2. therapeutic subgroup (e.g. L01: antineoplastic agents)
3. pharmacological subgroup (e.g. L01X: other antineoplastic agents)
4. chemical subgroup (e.g. L01XE: Protein kinase inhibitors)
5. chemical substance (e.g. L01XE05: Sorafenib[63])

The 4th ATC level is - even though the products within that group should not by default be considered "pharmacotherapeutically equivalent"[64] – providing an internationally accepted standard of similar products (a 'class') which can be used to analyze to which extent certain events of interest are associated with them. The following figure shows how the 4th ATC level can be selected in Empirica Signal. If a product is classified in more than one hierarchy, all appli-

---
[61] U.S. National Library of Medicine – MedlinePlus (2010), top.
[62] Norwegian Institute of Public Health (2011), 2.
[63] Norwegian Institute of Public Health (2011), 3.
[64] Norwegian Institute of Public Health (2011), 2.

cable categories can be selected stepwise. Acetylsalicylic acid for example can be found as analgesic and antipyretic with ATC code N02BA01[65] but also as antithrombotic agent with ATC code B01AC06[66].

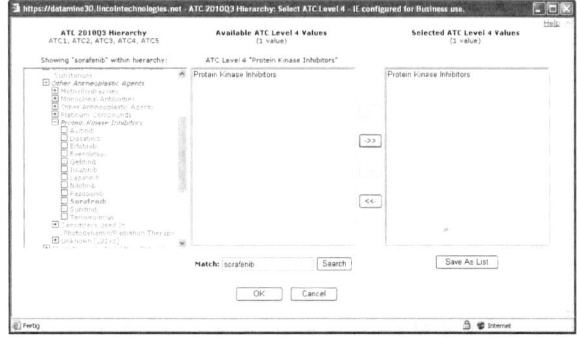

Figure 10: Selection of a ATC 4th level hierarchy in Empirica Signal.
Source: Own presentation using Empirica Signal.

Different to the product ATC code, the adverse event is already available with its path within MedDRA in the original source data from FDA and WHO and does not need to be coded by the software vendor. MedDRA "is a medical terminology used to classify adverse event information associated with the use of biopharmaceuticals and other medical products" to allow a standardized multilingual exchange and analysis of these data items[67]. The MedDRA dictionary is organized using five hierarchy levels:

- System Organ Class (SOC) (e.g. Gastrointestinal disorders),
- High-Level Group Terms (HLGT) (e.g. Gastrointestinal ulceration and perforation),
- High-Level Terms (HLT) (e.g. Intestinal ulcers and perforation NEC),
- Preferred Terms (PT) (e.g. Intestinal perforation) and
- Lower-Level Terms (LLT) (e.g. Bowel perforation)[68].

---

[65] Norwegian Institute of Public Health (2010), 1.
[66] Norwegian Institute of Public Health (2010), 2.
[67] MedDRA MSSO (2011), 1.
[68] Bayer Pharma MedDRA browser, see Annex I.

The PT is the lowest level that is available for analyses because the data between manufacturers and the FDA is exchanged on this level according to FDA guidelines.[69] In order to get an overview on other events for the review as well it is reasonable to use the next higher hierarchy level HLT as a selection parameter. The following figure shows how the HLT can be selected within Empirica Signal using the PT which is investigated as search parameter.

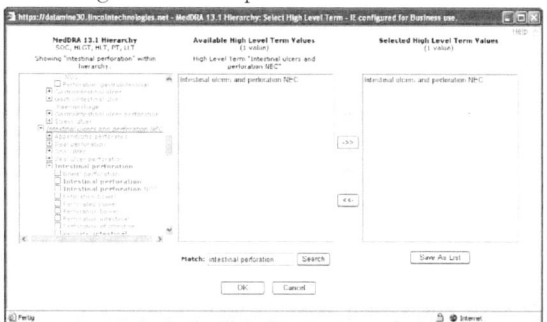

Figure 11: Selection of a HLT value in Empirica Signal.
Source: Own presentation using Empirica Signal.

The MedDRA dictionary is supplemented with Standardized MedDRA Queries (SMQs). Such queries group different MedDRA terms which belong to a "defined medical condition or area of interest".[70] Since they are established and maintained by medical experts (CIOMS SMQ Working Group) it is preferable to use SMQs rather than the HLT for grouping whenever a SMQ exists for the medical condition that is under investigation. Whether it exists can be checked by searching e.g. the PT in question in the SMQ definitions that are available on the Maintenance and Support Services Organization (MSSO) website or the Empirica Signal online help (MedDRA version release notes section). The figure below shows how a SMQ can be selected in Empirica Signal using the 'available values' button and 'containing' search.

---

[69] United States Food and Drug Administration (2008), 2, p.7.
[70] MedDRA MSSO (2011), 2.

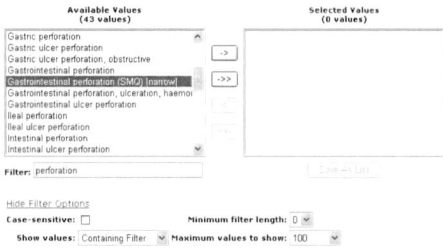

Figure 12:   SMQ selection in Empirica Signal.
Source: Own presentation using Empirica Signal.

The following chapters will systematically walk through the available reports within Empirica Signal. All reports will be analyzed regarding their suitability to provide additional or comprehensive information regarding the drug safety signal that is discussed and regarding their potential to answer the common questions that are raised by the medical reviewers. Any report that is meeting these requirements and presumably adds value to the medical discussion will be proposed to be included into the standard review package if is assumed to be beneficial in the majority of DECs that will later go through this assessment process. As every signal is potentially medically unique and therefore needs unique handling, beyond the standard set of queries, certain signals might raise more complex medical questions that can still be adequately supported by data from external databases. The reports that are subsequently evaluated might not become part of the standard package but could be used in such queries that arise in a second step. To support this, the reports will also be discussed in regards to the scenario where they become valuable. The additional questions might also be more precisely answered by selecting rougher or closer MedDRA or ATC level choices. The discussion above shows, that there is a variety of options what the optimal granularity level for the product and event could be. The ATC 4 and MedDRA HLT level will be used as a standard during the following review of available reports. Comparisons with other level choices will be made where appropriate, to demonstrate the influence of the selection on the results.

5.1.3. Product Related Reports

This chapter will discuss the available reporting options within Empirica Signal focusing on the drug component of the DEC under investigation. The application scenario the tool was built for was to determine signal scores within a certain dataset for a DEC. This resulted in a method simple to be used in the 'Data Mining

Results' menu as soon as the search strategy is determined. The figure below shows the input parameters that are used for the example AE and product. The HLT is used here even though a SMQ is available to be able to see the difference between both approaches in the following analysis. Besides the ATC and MedDRA value and level the underlying dataset (so called data mining run) needs to be selected. '2010Q3 Generic (S)' is the default set for the FDA AERS data containing data up to September 2010 including calculations for the SMQs. Run details can be displayed for every data mining run that is available in Empirica Signal. Alternatively there is the option to set filter criteria on these details and have only matching data mining runs displayed.

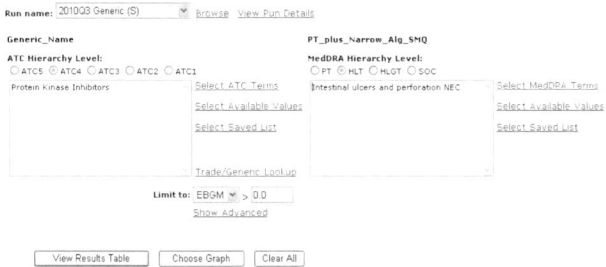

Figure 13: Basic Data Mining Results search configuration.
Source: Own presentation using Empirica Signal.

With these input parameters it is intended to demonstrate the statistical relationship between all drugs classified as Protein Kinase Inhibitors and all AEs that are classified as Intestinal ulcers and perforation 'not elsewhere classified' (NEC). The relationship is based on the reported AEs that the FDA had available on its database end of September 2010. Any statistically unexpected result will become manifest in EBGM or PRR scores that exceed the respective threshold and will draw the reviewers attention. In this example the DEC Sorafenib & Intestinal perforation has an EBGM score of 3.17 which means, that 3 times more AEs as expected have been reported, compared with the distribution of AEs on the FDA's database in general. Since the lower bound of the credible interval exceeds 1, the result can be regarded as statistically relevant.

When showing the results table the signal scores are displayed immediately for every generic name being classified by the selected ATC level code for which at least one Adverse Event was reported (PT of the relating HLT). By default, the results table contains a large number of columns. They have been set as a standard by the vendor to enable users to get a complete overview on the strongest statistical DEC associations on a given database. Controversially, in the discussion of a particular DEC, the majority is either part of the input parameters, related information (as e.g. the complete ATC or MedDRA path) or statistical values that are not in the focus of the DEC analysis. Hence, the default column selection of the results table should be changed in a way that only the columns are displayed which are needed by the reviewer later. Additional columns that are displayed might distract the reviewer from the key information. Also, for all signal scores that are presented, guidance is needed how to interpret them. Ideally, there should be no redundant (e.g. the search parameter in the result set) or unnecessary information (e.g. a signal score that is not used or put into context later). The following figure compares the default column selection with a cleaned and sorted version which should rather be used as a standard if data should be presented to the reviewer table-wise.

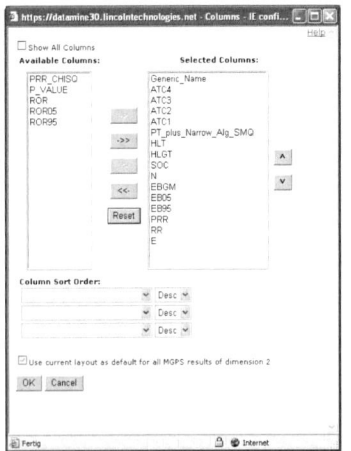
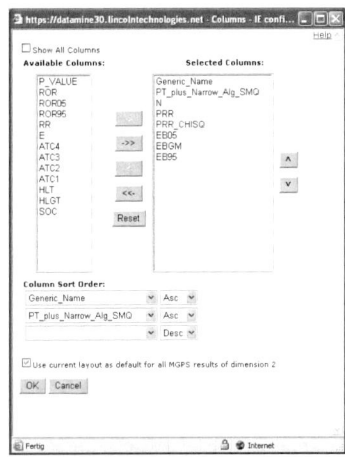

Figure 14: Default (left) vs. optimized (right) column selection for data mining results table.
Source: Own presentation using Empirica Signal.

Main modifications that were done, based on the previous considerations:
- Removal of the ATC and MedDRA path information
- Removal of other signal scores (E = expected reports, RR)
- Adding the Chi-square value of the PRR (because it is commonly used)
- Resorting of columns and result set to allow fluent reading

The reason for not adding the P-value of Chi-square is that both values are interrelated and when considering a P-value < 0.05 statistically significant this is already covered with Chi-square values above 3.84 (as described before, a Chi-square value of 4 is used as a threshold here)[71].

The result (see extract in the following table) shows the signal scores comprehensively for all 43 combinations, e.g. reports of Intestinal perforation during treatment with Sorafenib, that were reported at least once. The DEC Sorafenib and Intestinal perforation (highlighted red) can be found in 19 reports on the FDA AERS database which is exceeding the common signal score thresholds. The signal scores are also above these limits for another event within the same HLT (Large intestine perforation – colored blue) and for the same event but another drug within the same ATC 4 level (e.g. Sunitinib).

Generic_Name	PT_plus_Narrow_Alg_SMQ	N	PRR	PRR_CHISQ	EB05	EBGM	EB95
Pazopanib	Intestinal perforation	4	20.1	54.6	1.38	3.24	7.03
Pazopanib	Large intestine perforation	1	7.50	1.01	0.259	1.12	3.52
Sorafenib	Ileal perforation	1	4.95	0.434	0.212	0.920	2.88
Sorafenib	Intestinal perforation	19	6.50	82.3	2.15	3.17	4.53
Sorafenib	Large intestinal ulcer	2	2.28	0.437	0.310	0.958	2.40
Sorafenib	Large intestine perforation	17	8.72	107.4	2.30	3.47	5.06
Sorafenib	Small intestinal perforation	3	5.60	7.16	0.652	1.68	3.72
Sunitinib	Intestinal perforation	46	11.9	439.4	4.79	6.16	7.85
Sunitinib	Jejunal perforation	1	15.3	2.80	0.283	1.23	3.86
Sunitinib	Large intestine perforation	15	5.74	53.6	1.85	2.86	4.26
Sunitinib	Small intestinal perforation	5	7.02	19.9	1.12	2.37	4.54

Table 1: Extract of data mining results in FDA AERS Q3 2010 for HLT Intestinal ulcers and perforation NEC and ATC4 Protein Kinase Inhibitors.
Source: Own presentation using Empirica Signal.

The same methods can be applied using the VigiBase data as a source during the search definition. This allows to get the same figures calculated for a comparison. When the same methods for calculating the signal scores are used also on the company's database it allows to check if the signal of disproportionality is equal, weaker or stronger using a different background population. It also gives the opportunity to compare other products of the same class regarding the same type of

---

[71] Penn State Lehigh Valley University (2010), bottom.

adverse events. Chapter 5.1.7 will describe the advantages and disadvantages to combine the output of both databases into one single report.

Empirica Signal provides multiple pre-defined data mining runs besides the standard set of signal score calculations across all underlying data. One pre-configured evaluation strategy is to calculate the signal scores multiple times for cumulative data subsets separated by year. This allows to see the signal score trend over the past years until now together with other information such as e.g. the number of reports that have been reported until a certain year or the credible interval that was calculated in that period. The figure below shows how the parameter selection needs to be performed in Empirica Signal and how the columns need to be adapted in order to be able to review signal score trends.

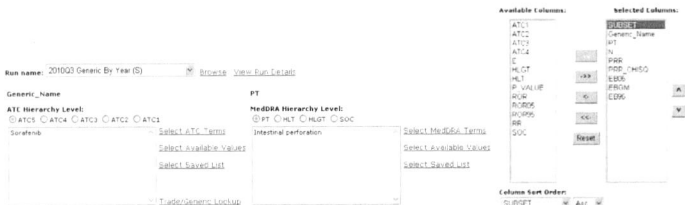

Figure 15: Selection of data mining run search and display parameter for a subset analysis per year.
Source: Own presentation using Empirica Signal.

The analysis in this example was performed on the exact DEC, i.e. on ATC 5 level (Sorafenib) in combination with the preferred term (Intestinal Perforation). The reason behind is that the trend analysis with broader selection of drugs and events with its scores is containing too much data items to be displayed in a table comprehensively because the time period is acting as a third dimension. The two following tables show the development of the signal scores on the FDA AERS and WHO VigiBase database.

SUBSET	Generic_Name	PT	N	PRR	PRR_CHISQ	EB05	EBGM	EB95
[1968-96]-[2006]	Sorafenib	Intestinal perforation	5	12.2	40.5	1.37	2.92	5.67
[1968-96]-[2007]	Sorafenib	Intestinal perforation	7	8.84	41.0	1.63	3.08	5.44
[1968-96]-[2008]	Sorafenib	Intestinal perforation	12	9.57	83.2	2.43	3.97	6.23
[1968-96]-[2009]	Sorafenib	Intestinal perforation	15	7.62	79.2	2.30	3.56	5.32
[1968-96]-[2010]	Sorafenib	Intestinal perforation	19	6.50	82.3	2.16	3.18	4.56

Table 2: Example DEC analysis on FDA AERS database (data set as of Q3 2010).
Source: Own presentation using Empirica Signal.

SUBSET	Generic_Name (Abridged)	PT	N	PRR	PRR_CHISQ	EB05	EBGM	EB95
1968-2005	Sorafenib	Intestinal perforation	2	50.6	53.9	0.613	2.02	5.77
1968-2006	Sorafenib	Intestinal perforation	3	14.8	25.9	0.813	2.12	4.75
1968-2007	Sorafenib	Intestinal perforation	5	13.5	46.0	1.35	2.88	5.62
1968-2008	Sorafenib	Intestinal perforation	8	8.66	46.6	1.63	2.96	5.06
1968-2009	Sorafenib	Intestinal perforation	13	9.68	92.1	2.34	3.74	5.76
1968-2010	Sorafenib	Intestinal perforation	16	9.83	117.4	2.66	4.06	6.02
1968-2011	Sorafenib	Intestinal perforation	16	9.36	110.6	2.59	3.95	5.84

Table 3: Example DEC analysis on VigiBase (data set as of Q1 2011).
Source: Own presentation using Empirica Signal.

With more reports being available cumulatively on the database the credible interval is getting smaller which means that the estimated disproportionality ratio is getting more precise and has fever random influences on the statistical values. This can be seen in the tables above but easier to understand and remember is a graphical representation of the data which can be easily created using for example the High-Low-Close chart in Microsoft Excel. For the given example the charts from both VigiBase and FDA AERS can be found below presenting the PRR for Sorafenib and Intestinal perforation on the left and the EBGM scores on the right scale.

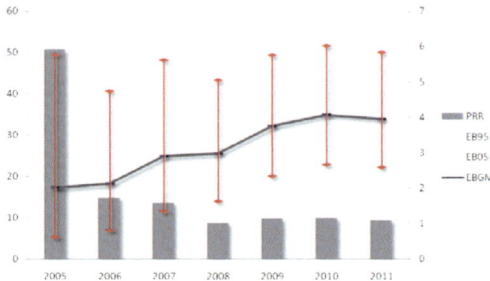

Figure 16: Signal scores trend analysis for the example DEC on VigiBase.
Source: Own presentation.

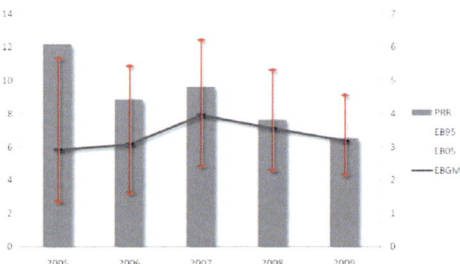

Figure 17: Signal scores trend analysis for the example DEC on FDA AERS.
Source: Own presentation.

As already discussed, the data items are calculated on for the concrete DEC Sorafenib & Intestinal perforation. However, there might be a good reason to compare the score development across multiple drugs (e.g. 4th ATC level) events (e.g. HLT level) or even databases in one chart. For the latter option a comparison chart can be found in chapter 5.1.7. In any case these analyses can be done only by displaying not more than one score to not overload the chart with information. If a SMQ is available and the time based review of cumulative subsets should happen for the complete SMQ scope a custom data mining run needs to be created. This is because SMQs in general are not part of the standard configuration for the subset data mining run. When creating a custom date mining run it is essential that the configuration is as close to the standard run as possible and deviates only where absolutely necessary to not lose comparability with other runs. Since it is sufficient to create the custom runs only once per quarter and the result can be re-used for all DECs which are evaluated a consistency check for custom data mining runs by a second person or any other review mechanism can be implemented with acceptable effort.

The plain signal score values that have been pulled from the databases at the beginning of this chapter can be displayed graphically in a variety of ways using standard Empirica Signal graphs to ease the data review. Bar graphs are most prominent here and can be used to visualize the two major signal scores (EBGM and PRR) for each associated event per drug that is available in the table result set. Another statistical value, the Reporting Odds Ratio (ROR), can also be used. But as it is playing a minor role in the reviewed literature it will not be further evaluated. The figure below shows the EBGM values from VigiBase (data as of Q1 2011) as a bar graph for two example products of the example 4th ATC level – Sorafenib and Sunitinib (for the other drugs within the same ATC level see annex II).

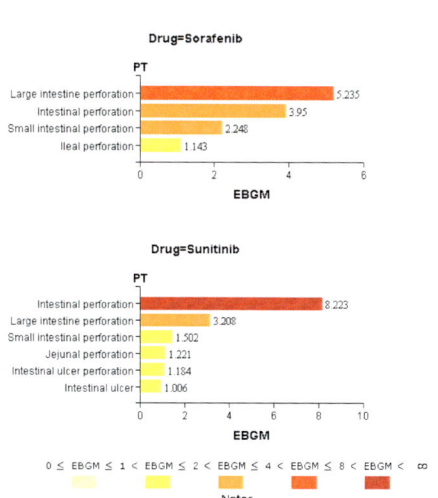

Figure 18: Example EBGM bar graph from VigiBase (Q1 2011) for Sorafenib and Sunitinib.
Source: Own presentation using Empirica Signal.

The DEC Sorafenib and Intestinal perforation is associated with an EBGM score of 3.95 in VigiBase – Large intestine perforation however shows an even stronger association considering the reporting disproportionality. Compared to Sunitinib the data shows that the same events are also more frequently reported as expected and Intestinal perforation is even associated with a EBGM score of 8.223. Both events Intestinal perforation and Large intestine perforation have exceeded the thresholds on the company database (see figure 31). The given bar graphs display comprehensively that the signal of disproportionate reporting can also be found in VigiBase and that other comparable events are showing up. Also the reported events can easily be compared with other drugs of the same drug class. The main advantage of these types of graphs is, that they can be created directly within the implemented tool without the need of exporting the raw data and any extra steps. For proper documentation the notes section should always be enabled before the printout or save to allow for example repeatability. The notes provide detailed information on what was the underlying data mining run and which database search or configuration items have been set.

A disadvantage of the basic bar graph is, that additional attributes of a DEC can only be made visible when moving the mouse over the respective bar within the tool. This option is as a matter of fact not available when the report is exported or printed. Since the additional information such as the credible interval is, as discussed in earlier chapters, very important and the previous example EBGM graph is very basic a more advanced bar graph can be used alternatively. As the following figure will show, the additional display of the credible interval is not adding too much complexity to the graph. The number of reports N can be optionally displayed as well. On one hand this figure is not needed from a statistical point of view since the EBGM calculation uses shrinkage mechanisms and the score itself is the key information. On the other hand the count integrates nicely into the graph and is useful information. An important configuration aspect is to have the bar color controlled by the EB05 and not by the EBGM since this is basically the only way to differentiate if the lower bound of the credible interval is below or above 1, which is often used as threshold suggesting statistical significance. The figure below shows the same example DEC with its signal scores from VigiBase as in the previous simple bar graph now with more details. The items which are set for the configuration are displayed as well.

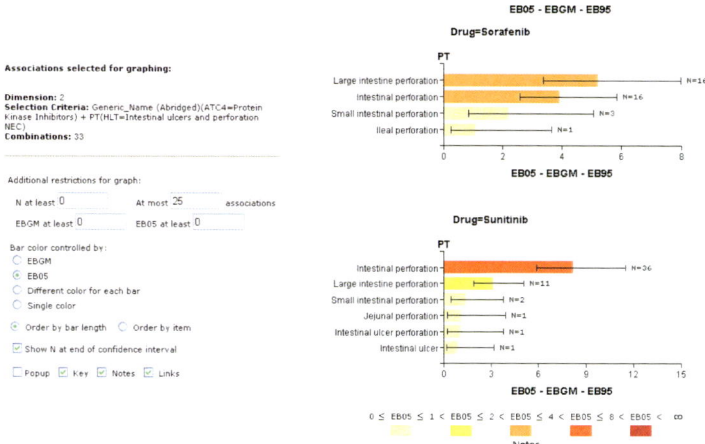

Figure 19: Example EBGM bar graph with credible intervals from VigiBase (Q1 2011) for Sorafenib and Sunitinib.
Source: Own presentation using Empirica Signal.

5.1.4. Event Related Reports

Similar to the bar graphs that are showing all selected adverse events that are related to a medicinal product the data mining result data set can also be shown in bar graphs per event by Empirica Signal. This view on the DEC is useful to review how comparable products are associated with the adverse event that is under investigation.

Again, there are two general choices, one regarding the complexity of the graph (driven by the number of displayed values) and one regarding the leading algorithm that is used for the disproportionality analysis. Since the ROR is playing a minor role only, the following example bar graph is showing both outputs for the PRR and EBGM to demonstrate the difference the statistical shrinkage makes for this example.

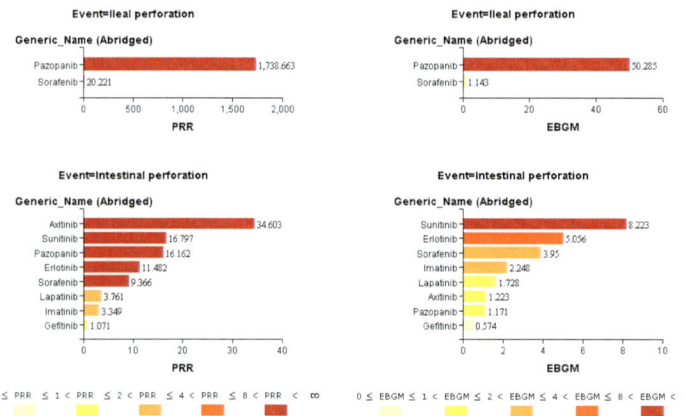

Figure 20: PRR and EBGM comparison concerning Ileal / Intestinal perforation and Protein Kinase Inhibitors.
Source: Own presentation using Empirica Signal.

For the adverse event or PT Intestinal perforation Pazopanib is associated with a PRR of above 16. The comparison with the EBGM score shows a major difference since the EBGM is only 1.17. Displaying this difference in the graph which is ordered descending by PRR and EBGM score of the associated product, Pazopanib is moved from the 3rd to the 7th row. The underlying reason is that there was only one report found in VigiBase for this DEC.

Similar to the bar graphs per product the more detailed version with credible intervals (see example below) displays this important additional information as well without overloading the chart. The reviewer's attention is directed to the statistically more confident associations using this approach rather than the simple bar graph (especially for PRR only).

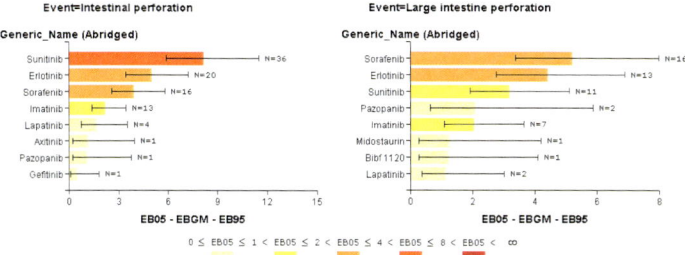

Figure 21: **Bar graph with credible intervals for two example events from VigiBase (Q1 2011).**
Source: Own presentation using Empirica Signal.

The very light yellow bars do not exceed 1 for the EB05 and hence are not qualified as a signal of disproportionate reporting using the commonly applied thresholds.

When calculating the signal scores for all PTs within a MedDRA HLT the event related bar graphs are created per event and so multiple charts need to be reviewed. If a SMQ for the medical concept under analysis is available, the bar graphs per event are suddenly reduced to just one which makes the review very comprehensive. A higher level review (e.g. SMQ, HLT) in general can help to bring up DECs that have not exceeded the thresholds in the quantitative analyses because for example the 3rd case is still missing.

Unfortunately, SMQ definitions are available only in FDA AERS data mining runs by default. In order to display the information on any other data source (e.g. VigiBase) the option 'PT Plus Narrow Alg SMQ' has to be added when creating a new data mining run. Only then a comparison between the FDA AERS and the VigiBase data is possible for the complete SMQ. The example below is a comparison of the SMQ signal scores from the FDA AERS(left) and VigiBase (right) data.

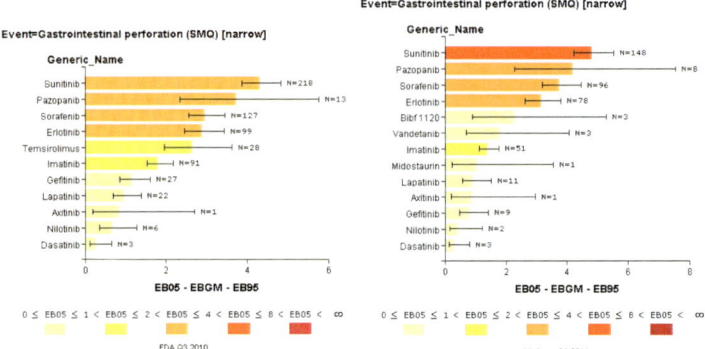

Figure 22: Comparison of bar graphs with credible intervals using the SMQ 'Gastrointestinal perforation' on FDA AERS (left) and VigiBase (right) data.
Source: Own presentation using Empirica Signal.

If no SMQ is available then there is one option in Empirica Signal to have the signal scores calculated for the complete HLT (or even higher) group instead for each PT within that group individually. The advantage is, that a drug comparison as in the previous bar graph can be created having just one score for the complete set of adverse events. In order to do so a new data mining run needs to be created which is using the HLT instead of the PT level for calculation. Any other grouping of events, for example company internal lists of MedDRA PTs that belong together is not possible with the standard Empirica Signal configuration.

If a SMQ is available all discussed analyses on HLT level can be replaced or supplemented by the individual PTs of the SMQ definition. In Empirica Signal the SMQ definitions for each MedDRA version are available in the online help. When entering the PTs via 'copy & paste' into the user interface the PTs containing a comma (e.g. Gastric ulcer perforation, obstructive) should be reviewed because they might not be recognized correctly since the comma is also the term separator. The result (see annex III) can become very large. An option here is to limit only to such DEC events where the EB05 is greater than 1 but then some events do not qualify to be displayed anymore. Then it is necessary to create a new data mining result, limited already to statistically significant associations in order to avoid any empty event records.

Listing the individual PTs of a SMQ is particularly helpful to address the question which events associated with a certain chemical entity should potentially become listed and will be included into e.g. CCDS and package information later.

5.1.5. Additional Reported Case Attributes

Besides the bar graphs with and without credible intervals Empirica Signal is offering tabular reports based on ICSRs to review the details of the cases. These 'case series' can be defined as underlying data for the report using a data mining result. However, if the result data set contains more than 20 rows (e.g. more than 20 DECs for a run on HLT and 4th ATC level) this approach is no longer possible. Alternatively the case series can be created using a query inside Empirica Signal and turn the result into a case series. The main difference between a data mining result and a query is that for the latter one no signal scores are calculated but rather all cases are selected that match a query definition. As the Sorafenib / Intestinal perforation query returns 43 DECs when defining the search as described the query wizard needs to be configured as shown in the figure below. The parameters HLT and ATC4 need to be chosen and filled with the given terms – by default both search parameters are combined using the 'AND' condition.

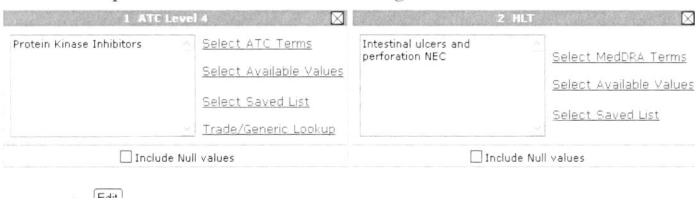

Figure 23: Example query wizard configuration for a DEC review case series creation.
Source: Own presentation using empirica signal.

The query wizard can also be used to search cases within the data mining runs using very complex search conditions. For the review of a DEC however it is sufficient to just have the same cases returned that are also showing up in the data mining results.

After creating a case series several standard reports can be run. These standard reports offer different case attributes to be either shown per case or as a percentage of all cases:

- Report Sources and Outcomes
- Report Type and Seriousness
- Route of Administration
- Drugs and Events
- Age Group and Gender
- Event MedDRA hierarchy

Most of these reports are helpful to get more knowledge about the case details and Empirica Signal offers to click on the cumulative numbers or case numbers to get the full case information that is available to the public. For a signal review however, most of these reports are already too detailed to be used in a standard report that is created for the medical expert.

One example report that is not available as a standard but can easily be created and is helpful for the review is a table that displays all reported adverse events according to the related PTs within the selected cases (and not only the PTs within the HLT group that was used for the selection of the case) together with its SOC as total number and percentage. The pre-configured report 'SOC [%]' can be used as a template by just adding the PT in question. Unfortunately, the display of the percentage of the respective PTs is not working any longer after this modification. If it still needs to be displayed the report can be exported into e.g. Microsoft Excel and the percentages can be calculated there. The table below shows a subset of the example result.

SOC	PT	N 1310	%
Blood	Anaemia	8	0,61%
Blood	Anaemia haemolytic autoimmune	1	0,08%
Blood	Bone marrow failure	1	0,08%
Blood	Coagulopathy	1	0,08%
Blood	Disseminated intravascular coagulation	9	0,69%
Blood	Febrile neutropenia	2	0,15%
Blood	Hilar lymphadenopathy	1	0,08%
Blood	Leukocytosis	1	0,08%
Blood	Leukopenia	3	0,23%
Blood	Lymphadenopathy	1	0,08%
Blood	Neutropenia	5	0,38%
Blood	Pancytopenia	3	0,23%
Blood	Splenic vein thrombosis	1	0,08%
Blood	Thrombocytopenia	11	0,84%
Blood	Thrombotic microangiopathy	1	0,08%
Card	Atrial fibrillation	2	0,15%
Card	Atrioventricular block first degree	1	0,08%
Card	Bradycardia	1	0,08%
Card	Cardiac arrest	2	0,15%

Figure 24: Percentage of single events in cases that contain the Sorafenib and Intestinal perforation.

Source: Own presentation.

An aggregation or count of other case attributes is potentially showing clusters of what was reported about the patients, the drugs or the events, but does not necessarily help to understand if there is a difference regarding the DEC in the signal scores that are calculated for reporting disproportionality in a certain subgroup. The standard report 'Age Group:Gender [N]' (tab. 4) shows the case count for each age group and gender combination. For demonstration purposes the same report was run for the DEC Terazosin & Urinary incontinence which is known to be a typical adverse event that is mainly affecting women.[72]

Age Group	Gender		
	Female Reports N	Male Reports N	Unknown Reports N
0 - 17	1	1	0
18 - 64	108	166	13
65 - above	71	127	7
Unknown	38	53	39

Protein Kinase Inhibitors + Gastrointestinal Perforation (SMQ)
FDA Q3 2010

Age Group	Gender		
	Female Reports N	Male Reports N	Unknown Reports N
0 - 17	0	1	0
18 - 64	36	10	1
65 - above	49	42	0
Unknown	40	16	7

Terazosin + Urinary incontinence
FDA Q3 2010

Table 4: Two example Age group / Gender standard reports.
Source: Own presentation using Empirica Signal.

The example of Terazosin in table 4 shows, that the majority of cases are reported for women. However, for the age group 65 years and above the case count is almost equal for both genders. The question that a review of a DEC with statistical methods on an external database can answer in this situation is, if there is a difference in e.g. the EBGM if it is calculated for males and females in the database separately.

In order to do so another custom data mining run needs to be created where suitable subgroups can be specified. Empirica Signal is not fully flexible in which case items of special interest can be used as subgroups but offers choices for gender and age which will be further discussed. Both case attributes are determining into which group one case will be put before a separate calculation takes place. The figure below illustrates how the database is divided using the age group as separator.

---

[72] Marshal, Beevers (1996), p.507.

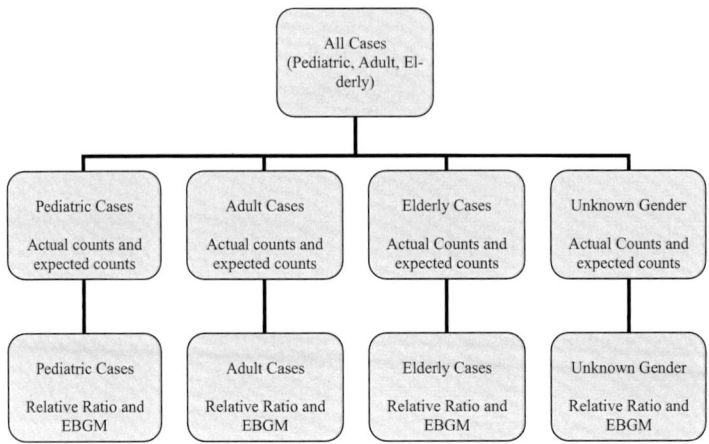

Figure 25: Signal score calculation tree for age subgroups.
Source: Own presentation using Empirica Online help " using a subset variable".

Additionally, every case where no age group can be assigned is put into the 'unknown' age group and signal scores are calculated for this one as well.

For the subset age group there are three options available within Empirica Signal:

- Agegroup9: unknown, 0-1, 2-4, 5-12, 13-16, 17-45, 46-75, 76-85, >85 years
- Agegroup4: unknown, 0-17, 18-64, 65 years and above
- Agegroup3: unknown, 0-64, 65 years and above.

The Agegroup3 is not considering the pediatric subgroup. Agegroup9 is too detailed for most analyses and at the same time not using common definitions of age groups – for example no scores for elderly can be calculated because this is normally defined as 65 years and above[73]. Agegroup9 can still be used for stratification purposes to give a more precise score if e.g. an endangered subgroup is underrepresented in the overall reporting.

For the gender there is just one subgroup definition that can be used, distinguishing between cases reported with patients of female, male or unknown gender.

---

[73] Norwegian Institute of Public Health (2011), 1.

A data mining run can not be configured in order to use two subgroup variables at the same time. Configuring two subgroup runs for each database is a one-time task only and can be used for all future analysis on the same dataset.

The tables below show the signal score values for Terazosin and Urinary incontinence. The tabular display is sufficient when searching for a given DEC. If scores are calculated for multiple drugs it is useful to use other graphical outputs that will be discussed later.

SUBSET	Generic_Name	PT_plus_Narrow_Alg_SMQ	N	PRR	PRR_CHISQ	EB05	EBGM	EB95
00_17	Terazosin	Urinary incontinence	1	55.5	12.9	0.348	1.46	4.67
18_64	Terazosin	Urinary incontinence	47	8.33	294.1	5.42	6.99	8.97
65_above	Terazosin	Urinary incontinence	91	8.01	536.8	5.04	6.03	7.19
UNK	Terazosin	Urinary incontinence	63	23.8	1318.8	16.9	21.0	25.7

Table 5: Terazosin / Urinary incontinence signal score calculation per age subgroup.
Source: Own presentation using Empirica Signal (data from FDA AERS as of Q3 2010).

SUBSET	Generic_Name	PT_plus_Narrow_Alg_SMQ	N	PRR	PRR_CHISQ	EB05	EBGM	EB95
F	Terazosin	Urinary incontinence	125	52.7	6186.1	35.9	41.7	48.2
M	Terazosin	Urinary incontinence	69	4.80	200.7	2.90	3.55	4.30
U	Terazosin	Urinary incontinence	8	9.85	54.2	2.63	4.91	8.65

Table 6: Terazosin / Urinary incontinence signal score calculation per gender subgroup.
Source: Own presentation using Empirica Signal (data from FDA AERS as of Q3 2010).

Compared to the pure case counts that have been drawn before (tab. 4) this table now shows an EBGM score for the female sub-population which is more than ten times higher as for males. Signal scores calculated for subgroups, based on this analysis, contain much more information than the number of reports alone since the strength of association of the DEC to the subgroup is also considered. Such an association could be missed or underestimated when the case count for the sub-population is low and scores are not calculated separately.

If the complete drug class (ATC level 4) is analyzed and more than one drug - event association is calculated at the same time the results can be displayed in a map graph by events to see the signal scores for a subset. In the example of Sorafenib and Intestinal perforation the SMQ Gastrointestinal perforation is used which reduces the number of events for the calculation to just one and subsequently limits the report to just one map graph per subgroup and external database. The standard Empirica Signal output is one report per subset gender and age group (see annex IV and annex V). Alternatively this can be arranged in one manual report which is more comprehensive as in the example figure below but is requiring additional work when it is prepared.

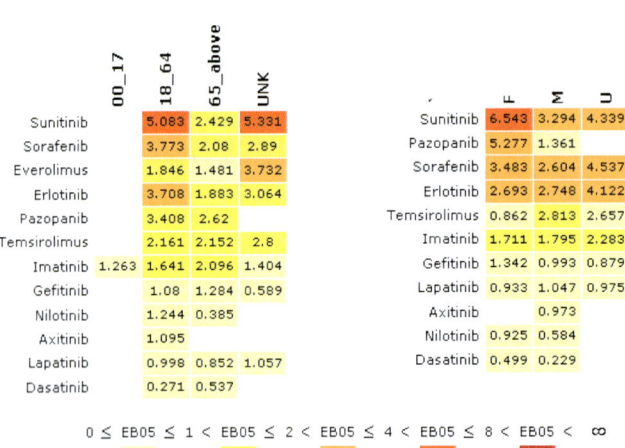

Figure 26: Example map graph for gender and age subgroups signal scores.
Source: Own presentation using Empirica Signal (data from FDA AERS as of Q3 2010).

The values displayed are the EBGM scores for the respective combination. The color is determined by the EB05 value in order to assess statistical significance at the same time. The number of reported events per DEC and subgroup is not displayed in this graph. In order to bring the statistical scores into a context at least the number of reports where no subgroup was assigned ('U' and 'UNK') would be required. Otherwise, the potential impact of the data quality in terms of completeness can not be properly assessed.

When no SMQ is available there are multiple scores for the distinct PTs within the HLT group which is looked at. Again, a standard run can be created on HLT level to create the scores for the complete HLT group which would lead to a similar output as for the SMQs. The detailed report per PT in the HLT group could then be provided additionally.

5.1.6. Three Dimensional (3D) Analysis

The previously described analyses were all based on two dimensional (2D) calculations using the medicinal product as one and the adverse event as the other dimension. For a data mining run all available pairs are checked for their frequency and compared with their statistically expected count based on the background population within the spontaneous reporting database to express the signal scores. Current computer hardware is already powerful enough to calculate all these scores within an acceptable timeframe and can perform calculations using even three dimensions. The third dimension can again be defined as a drug or event. As for the EBGM calculation the reported number of one combination can be compared to the expected number in order to come up with an EBGM score for the triplet. There are two types of associations possible:

- **Drug – Event – Drug** and
- **Drug – Event – Event** combinations.

Showing all DEC combinations with any co-reported product (suspect and concomitant drugs) separately and with their individual EBGM scores can help the medical reviewer to identify if any product is reported more often together with the DEC under investigation as it would be expected. A disproportionally high reporting rate could be the indicator for drug-drug interactions as well as for confounding by co-suspect or concomitant products. The interaction signal score (INTSS) can be computed as a statistical value for the strength of the 3D association compared to all related 2D associations. The INTSS is calculated by the EB05 of the triplet divided by the maximum EB95 of any combined pair within this triplet (e.g. the DEC only). An INTSS greater than one is a signal of disproportionate reporting of the triplet because then even its conservative signal score value is exceeding the upper bound of any 2D association[74].

Co-reported events could similarly point to confounding by indication or an underlying disease to explain a disproportionally high 2D signal score.

---

[74] Hauben (2007), p. 1145.

In Empirica Signal the 3D runs do not include SMQs by default and only consider combinations with a minimum count of five. A creation of a custom 3D run with a minimum count of one failed due to system limitations. Also the creation of a run including SMQ definitions failed even though a minimum adverse event count of five was used. The only alternative that worked was a custom run with SMQs not considering concomitant medication.

In order to evaluate if focusing on co-suspect products is sufficient a comparison of the pre-defined 3D run to a custom 3D run with suspect drugs only was done using a known drug-drug interaction example of Digoxin and Clarithromycin causing cardiac arrhythmia (PT = Arrhythmia)[75]. The 3D run with suspect and concomitant drugs return an EBGM score of 6.11 and an INTSS of 1.49. The 3D run with suspect drugs only did not return any signal score for this triplet because there are too few reports with this combination and both products are reported as suspect in the database. As a conclusion, the 3D runs need to consider concomitant medication as well. In order to achieve this for the following analyses the software vendor was contacted and asked to review the errors that were observed in the first runs and finally a 3D run with SMQs including suspect and concomitant drugs could be created. To give a rough estimate on the timing, the underlying calculations were performed in about 7 hours for the data mining run.

In general, there are three options to display 3D run results. The nested credible interval graph is showing the EBGM scores for the single associations and the combined one. In addition, every combination where the INTSS exceeds the value of one is highlighted in red. The following chart displays the suspect drugs that have been reported in cases with Sorafenib and one term of the SMQ Gastrointestinal perforation at least 5 times. All credible intervals overlap with at least one single 2D interval which means that there is no statistical signal for e.g. a potential interaction of the products in figure 27. The complete report (see annex VI) lists all products of the ATC level 4 to allow comparison. No INTSS score above 1 can be found here either.

---

[75] Wikimedia Foundation Inc. (2008).

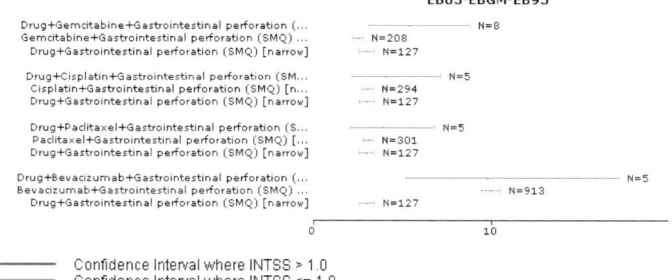

Figure 27: Nested credible interval for Sorafenib and SMQ Gastrointestinal perforation and any other suspect product.
Source: Own presentation using Empirica Signal (data from FDA AERS as of Q3 2010)

Compared to previous reports an association with Bevacizumab can be found which did not show up earlier because of a different ATC classification (but same 3rd ATC level 'other Antineoplastic Agents'). The chart nicely displays the count of events for Bevacizumab and the SMQ Gastrointestinal perforation and the EBGM credible interval of around ten which is already far above the Sorafenib value. Literature shows, that the risk of this adverse event is known to be elevated for patients treated with this medication[76].

Following the conclusion of the Digoxin and Clarithromycin example the same analysis was done considering both suspect and concomitant drugs. Far more associations can be found here. Figure 28 is displaying only the top 5 EBGM scores for the 3D analysis of Sorafenib (complete chart in annex VII).

---

[76] Hapani, Chu, Wu (2009), p.559.

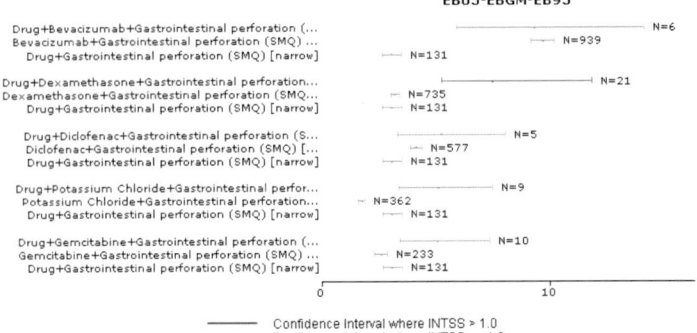

Figure 28: Nested credible interval for Sorafenib and SMQ Gastrointestinal perforation and any other suspect or concomitant product.
Source: Own presentation using Empirica Signal (data from FDA AERS as of Q3 2010).

In contrast to the previous analysis with additional suspect drugs, only one association with an INTSS exceeding 1 (1.53) can be found with Dexamethasone. The potential of interactions of Sorafenib and Dexamethasone can be found in the literature[77]. Because of the amount of associations with concomitant drugs the next 3D analysis results display option will consider suspect drugs only to evaluate their suitability.

As one of the remaining alternatives it is possible to display the 3D associations also per event (in this example for the SMQ Gastrointestinal perforation). This results in a graph difficult to read and interpret (see Annex VIII) but as the INTSS values are highlighted it can still be used since the most important information can not be missed. The way the graph presents the values is not very comprehensive but a major advantage of this representation is, that the INTSS concept can easily be followed by the reviewer.

A second method to display the 3D associations with the INTSS is the overlap graph per event. It shows the single product associations with the event and in addition the INTSS of the triplet. As the below example shows, this is a very com-

---

[77] Greil, Micksche (2006), p.11.

prehensive table and color highlighting of both, the EBGM and INTSS scores helps to identify strong associations easily. But compared to the nested credible interval graph it is less self explaining.

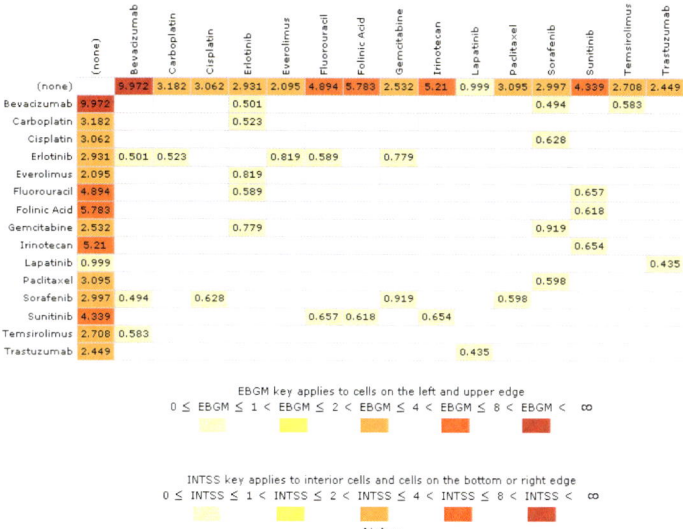

Figure 29: **Overlap graph for ATC (4th level) Protein Kinase Inhibitors and SMQ Gastrointestinal perforation.**
Source: Own presentation using Empirica Signal.

The third option for a report showing 3D associations is the hierarchy graph which is showing the 2D associations with the respective scores and then the combined INTSS score if a third variable (suspect drug or different event) is added. As the below example of the hierarchy graph shows the result is similar to the overlap graph but not as comprehensive since it is displayed per product of the ATC level whereas before all drugs were included in one overview. The credible intervals are not printed which is a deficiency if the result is to be printed or exported to a pdf document for further review.

Drug=Sorafenib

Item A	Drug + Item A (EBGM)	Item B	Drug + Item A + Item B (INTSS)
Bevacizumab		+ Gastrointestinal perforation (SMQ) [narrow]	0.494
Cisplatin		+ Gastrointestinal perforation (SMQ) [narrow]	0.628
Gastrointestinal perforation (SMQ) [narr...	2.997	+ Bevacizumab	0.494
		+ Cisplatin	0.628
		+ Gemcitabine	0.919
		+ Paclitaxel	0.598
Gemcitabine		+ Gastrointestinal perforation (SMQ) [narrow]	0.919
Paclitaxel		+ Gastrointestinal perforation (SMQ) [narrow]	0.598

EBGM key applies to cells in the left column
0 ≤ EBGM ≤ 1 < EBGM ≤ 2 < EBGM ≤ 4 < EBGM ≤ 8 < EBGM < ∞

INTSS key applies to cells in the right column
0 ≤ INTSS ≤ 1 < INTSS ≤ 2 < INTSS ≤ 4 < INTSS ≤ 8 < INTSS < ∞

Figure 30: Hierarchy graph for ATC (4th level) Protein Kinase Inhibitors and SMQ Gastrointestinal perforation.
Source: Own presentation using Empirica Signal.

Independence-model overlap graphs are also available in Empirica Signal. As per note of the software vendor this functionality is going to be discontinued in future versions of the tool and so it will not be evaluated further for report creation. It was the predecessor of the INTSS score model which is now used to analyze statistical 3D associations.

Three-dimensional signal scores calculated for Drug-Event-Event combinations will not be further evaluated in this study. The reason for that is the availability of SOC, PT [N,%] reports displaying all co-reported events in contrast to a 3D analysis where there would be a minimum of five cases required. Also, there was no literature found on how these particular 3D scores can be interpreted.

5.1.7. Comparison Overviews

As an addition to the reports that are offered by Empirica Signal it might be helpful for certain strategic decisions to create custom overviews of tables or charts which cover more than one database. Figure 22 already shows a custom built overview of the same analysis on the FDA and VigiBase data. Besides this option of just aligning similar graphs the information can be incorporated into one chart.

As an example the review of the signal score trend which was discussed could be done in one graph as shown below.

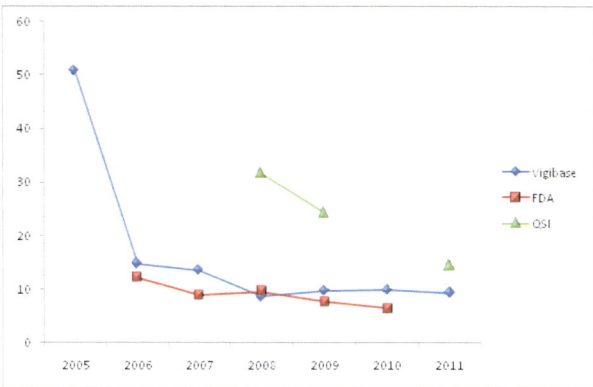

Figure 31: PRR review of Sorafenib and Intestinal perforation in a combined chart.
Source: Own presentation.

This chart is helpful to compare the own database (QSI) score development in the cumulative subsets against both external databases that are supported by Empirica Signal. The PRR was chosen as the value to be displayed because it was calculated for all three data sources. The single charts however show more details as e.g. the credible interval or the EBGM score which is essential information since these signal scores are all calculated using a statistical method and hence the full information set for the respective model needs to be reviewed at once ideally.
Alternatively every information that was calculated on one database can be exported to Microsoft Excel easily using Empirica Signal. After the export the scores of the different sources can be aligned by DEC. The Excel spreadsheet can be modified in a way that for the different scores the value itself is highlighted when it exceeds a certain threshold. As an example the signal scores for the 4th ATC level of Sorafenib and MedDRA HLT of Intestinal perforation have been incorporated into one example Excel spreadsheet with highlighting (using red font) the single scores per configured threshold. The DEC itself is colored red when all thresholds are exceeded at the same time on both external databases (some DECs might be found on one database only).

			FDA Q3 2010						Vigibase Q1 2011					OSI 2011		
Generic_Name	PT	N	PRR	PRR_CHISQ	EB05	EBGM	EB95	N	PRR	PRR_CHISQ	EB05	EBGM	EB95	N	PRR	PRR_CHISQ
Axitinib	Small intestine ulcer	2	695.73	486.76	0.772	3.437										
Dasatinib	Intestinal ulcer	1	4.39	0.324	0.278	1.205		2	11.131	9.668	0.632	2.039				
Dasatinib	Large intestinal ulcer	4	15.149	39.42	1.39	3.131		2	9.69	1.52	0.244	1.094				
Erlotinib	Intestinal perforation	23	9.187	158.144	3.191	4.524		20	11.482	179.529	3.47	5.056				
Erlotinib	Large intestinal ulcer	2	2.654	0.736	0.332	1.026		1	3.889	0.228	0.191	0.856				
Erlotinib	Large intestine perforation	12	7.754	57.073	1.771	2.881		13	21.502	230.271	2.763	4.443				
Erlotinib	Small intestinal perforation	3	6.536	9.095	0.699	1.801		4	12.043	10.611	0.504	1.595				
Erlotinib	Small intestine ulcer	2	13.698	12.335	0.578	1.79		1	19.216	3.794	0.256	1.151				
Gefitinib	Ileal perforation	1	7.691	1.044	0.261	1.132										
Gefitinib	Ileal ulcer	1	9.35	1.41	0.269	1.166										
Gefitinib	Intestinal perforation	3	1.584	0.193	0.333	0.859		1	1.079	0.202	0.128	0.574				
Gefitinib	Large intestinal ulcer	4	7.094	15.111	0.871	1.996										
Gefitinib	Large intestine perforation	1	1.579	0.043	0.23	0.71										
Gefitinib	Small intestinal perforation	2	2.891	0.068	0.208	0.903										
Imatinib	Intestinal perforation	17	3.918	30.603	1.547	2.328		13	11.277	1.896	0.246	1.106	3.511			
Imatinib	Intestinal ulcer	3	2.687	1.703	0.684	1.762		3	3.349	19.024	1.407	2.248	1.186			
Imatinib	Large intestine ulcer	2	2.306	1.099	0.391	1.008		3	3.02	2.272	0.713	1.857	3.61			
Imatinib	Large intestine perforation	9	3.099	10.708	0.929	1.629		7	5.177	1.506	0.382	1.199	3.608			
Imatinib	Small intestinal perforation	5	6.533	17.218	1.112	2.391				19.302	1.097	2.076				
Lapatinib	Intestinal perforation	6	2.883	5.516	0.832	1.648		4	3.761	5.573	0.749	1.728				
Lapatinib	Large intestine perforation	1	0.712	0.007	0.109	0.474		2	5.391	3.416	0.379	1.189				
Lapatinib	Small intestinal perforation	2	6.232	3.25	0.491	1.517		1	9.085	1.564	0.24	1.077				
Nilotinib	Ileal perforation	1	21.15	4.796	0.286	1.243										
Nilotinib	Intestinal perforation	1	1.588	0.027	0.166	0.72										
Nilotinib	Intestinal ulcer	1	5.316	0.516	0.25	1.081										
Nilotinib	Large intestine ulcer	1	42.165	9.447	0.303	1.322										
Pazopanib	Ileal perforation	1	73.099	17.174	0.302	1.317		3	1739.7	3455.351	2.534	50.29	194.06			
Pazopanib	Intestinal perforation	4	20.079	54.603	1.309	3.241		4	16.162	3.102	0.26	1.171	1.79			
Pazopanib	Large intestine perforation	1	4.501	1.008	0.259	1.134		2	99.013	100.57	0.649	2.139	5.693			
Sorafenib	Ileal perforation	1	4.946	0.434	0.212	0.92		1	20.221	4.037	0.254	1.143	3.168			
Sorafenib	Intestinal perforation	19	6.497	82.28	2.191	3.16		16	9.346	110.586	2.508	3.95	5.645	10	14.47	94.55
Sorafenib	Large intestine perforation	2	2.276	0.437	0.31	0.958	1.69										
Sorafenib	Large intestine perforation	17	8.221	107.41	2.395	3.469		16	27.139	369.52	3.396	5.235		11	12.87	129.45
Sorafenib	Small intestinal perforation	4	5.606	7.156	0.652	1.679		4	18.536	33.306	0.86	2.248	5.599			
Sunitinib	Intestinal perforation	46	11.9	439.415	4.744	6.162		36	16.797	511.175	5.925	8.223	11.506			
Sunitinib	Jejunal perforation	1	15.284	2.799	0.283	1.228		1	62.017	13.689	0.271	1.221	4.104			
Sunitinib	Large intestine perforation	15	5.743	53.501	1.85	2.858		11	14.645	124.806	1.906	3.208	5.524			
Sunitinib	Small intestinal perforation	5	7.016	19.075	1.125	2.374		2	9.718	8.059	0.478	1.502	3.826			
Temsirolimus	Ileal ulcer perforation	6	117.807	27.206	0.312	1.376										
Temsirolimus	Intestinal perforation	6	8.836	34.151	1.433	2.844										
Temsirolimus	Intestinal ulcer perforation	2	63.74	12.345	0.308	1.351										
Temsirolimus	Large intestine perforation	1	4.4	2.402	0.409	1.364										
Temsirolimus	Small intestinal perforation	1	8.054	1.134	0.254	1.102										
Axitinib	Intestinal perforation							1	34.603	7.679	0.271	1.223				
Blbf 1120	Large intestine perforation							1	117.03	28.233	0.278	1.262	4.065			
Midostaurin	Large intestine perforation							1	175.54	42.842	0.281	1.285				
Sunitinib	Intestinal ulcer							1	1.799	0.006	0.224	1.006				
Sunitinib	Intestinal ulcer perforation							1	7.889	1.083	0.263	1.184				

Table 7: Signal Score Analysis for Sorafenib and Intestinal perforation.
Source: Own presentation.

5.2. Proposal on Standard Report Package

5.2.1. Output Preparation and Customization

The manually created custom tables or graphs are helpful for the review and the resulting decisions because they show the most relevant information comprehensively. However, since these reports are used for scientific review within a pharmaceutical company the time needed for the preparation of custom reports or graphs should not outweigh the additional value. The important report creation steps, as well as switches set during the preparation phase, need to be documented. This is possible in Empirica Signal with printing the 'Notes' at the end of each report. For custom results it must be ensured that the process of export, preparation and presentation is not modifying the data in any way. These validation efforts are time and cost-intensive as the documentation which is created needs to be inspection-ready. In this light the additional benefit for the reviewer is significantly reduced, looking into the example custom reports that have been created for Sorafenib and Intestinal perforation.

Some of the analyses that were made required a custom creation of a data mining run to include e.g. SMQs into the signal score calculation. Since these runs can be re-used for the upcoming DEC evaluations it is essential that the initial configuration of these runs is completely documented. This is also mainly because, as the results in section 5.1. have pointed out, the configuration switches that are available (e.g. suspect drugs only vs. suspect and concomitant drugs) make a significant difference in the associations that are found and are finally made available for the review. Additionally, wherever possible and reasonable the standard data mining runs should be used in order to be able to compare results with any analysis that is potentially performed by other parties such as regulatory authorities. Any modification to a standard data mining run should be carefully revisited as experiences with the results are gathered. Custom data mining runs used in chapter 5.1. for analyses that are proposed to be kept or created per external database for use in standard reports are:

- a 3D data mining run with suspect and concomitant drugs including SMQs,
- a data mining run with SMQs and subset gender,
- a data mining run with SMQs and subset age,
- a data mining run with SMQs and cumulative subset by year.

5.2.2. Standard Outputs

In order to avoid the additional validation and documentation efforts for the creation of custom reports and because of the low additional value which would in contrast be gained it is proposed to use the direct outputs from Empirica Signal wherever possible. This eliminates the option of a graphical presentation of the signal score development over the past years as in figure 16 and 17 but can be created from the tabular presentation by the reviewer if needed.

The output format should exclusively be the portable document format (pdf) to avoid any accidental modification of the data. This is supported by Empirica Signal for all results. As an exception for tables the export into Microsoft Excel is recommended to ease the review by delivering filter and enhanced search options. In the interest of consistency and 'auditability' a copy of the delivered package needs to stay with the creating party as documentation. To allow reproducibility all standard outputs must contain a documentation of the parameters used to create the tables or graphs (e.g. data mining run that was used, product selection, event selection, sub-grouping, etc). Normally this can be achieved by adding the 'Notes' section by default to the output. Furthermore a standard explanation page describing the statistical methods PRR, Chi2, CI, EBGM and (if used) applied thresholds should be part of the standard package to guide the reviewer through the interpretation of the presented values.

From a scientific standpoint the default selection of the products and events that are included into the review should be on a meaningful next higher level than the DEC itself. For analyses created by a company to verify a signal of disproportionate reporting however, there is a management decision needed what will happen to the information gained on other events or drugs. In this regulated environment it is therefore proposed to use the PT and 5th ATC level for the analysis only. Any broader search on e.g. SMQ or HLT level for events and similarly on the 4th ATC level is recommended as optional or follow-up analysis only under these circumstances.

As a summary of the valuable reports analyzed in section 5.1., the following reports are proposed to be generated into a standard package per external database for the purpose of signal verification:

1. The **tabular listing of the signal scores** displaying the EBGM, PRR, PRR Chi Square, EB05, EB95 and the number of reported events per DEC to get a first overview on the signal scores on the external database. If the company's internal algorithm calculates a different score which is supported (e.g. ROR) this score should be added to the listing.
2. A **tabular signal score trend** listing for the DEC under investigation on the cumulative subset per year for a review of the signal score development.
3. The **bar graph using EBGM with credible interval by product** to have a graphical representation of the scores from the tabular listing. If a SMQ is available then the presentation should display the scores for all single PTs the SMQ covers. If multiple products are analyzed but the analysis is focussing on a single PT only then the bar graph with credible interval should be displayed by event to be able to view the scores for this event for drugs of the same class comprehensively.
4. One **table for gender and** one for **age subgroups** signal scores to see if there is a higher statistical association in a certain subgroup. The reason not to display the associated map graph here is for evaluation purposes; the information how big the quantity of cases classified with unknown gender or age is can not be displayed but is nevertheless very valuable
5. The **nested credible interval graph** generated **from the 3D data mining result per product** for the evaluation of e.g. interactions. This report however needs again consideration regarding what will be done with the results and hence needs management approval.
6. A **report** of the type **SOC:PT [N]** (with inclusion of the percentage as soon as supported) on the case series created from the tabular listing in order to be able to see other events that have been reported in the cases that are reviewed.

As of today an external database review for SDRs is not part of the review process at the Bayer Pharma AG. Hence, the proposal itself should be reviewed after sufficient experience with the generated reports was gained. Also the related scientific platforms should be actively monitored to include newly arising trends in signal detection or signal review into the company's approach.

5.3. Identified Gaps and Possible Enhancements

During the assessment of the standard features and outputs of Empirica Signal it was found that there are several ways to display the same facts from different perspectives. Where some are more intuitively to understand for the evaluation of a given DEC others might show their real potential in signal detection rather than in signal investigation. It was found to be essential that all reports dealing with scores of statistical reporting disproportionality need to show all relevant values (or alternatively color highlighted when thresholds are exceeded) that are normally used to determine statistical significance. Since several reports were not configurable for these items they were not proposed to be used in a standard package. Some reports allow making the missing values visible when moving the cursor over the respective item within the application. But this feature can of course not be used when the result is printed.

Ideally, more standard runs including SMQs and subsets age and gender should be pre-configured in order to avoid any inconsistency. The same holds true for 3D runs that are certainly very complex but should be pre-configured with SMQs and a minimum count of 3 (as this is a commonly used threshold). Alternatively, free configurable data mining runs should work without system limitations. Any restriction made here reduces the chance to find free associations for e.g. interactions or is eliminating the chance to re-use the same data mining run for the next analysis.

The standard reports on case series can be fully used but as shown for the example modification to display a SOC, PT [N,%] report the customization is not fully supported.

To increase comprehensiveness a combination report using both external databases for the creation of reports that can be immediately compared would be helpful as well. Still, since the majority of questions addressed in the above chapters could be answered the available reports are sufficient to generate a report for medical expert reviews.

Additional reports that could have been created but which are not supported by Empirica Signal are data mining runs that calculate scores by more than one subgroup at the same time. Also 3D runs that can use other items than drug or adverse event in the third dimension could allow further room for exploration. Items like product indication, concomitant disease, patient weight or other case attributes could be used as free variables in order to detect clusters or risk factors for the given DEC.

6. Future Work and Conclusions

The analysis of available reports within Empirica Signal has shown that the tool provides a variety of options to validate a signal of disproportionate reporting on both external databases that are most commonly used. The proposed reports can be created in about half an hour time when the data mining runs are updated every 3 months. As benefit a statistical signal score from the company's internal adverse event database can be compared to the scores based on the FDA or VigiBase data easily and provides a statistical second opinion to evaluate the hypotheses of that association. This opinion can generally be regarded as statistically more relevant since the external databases contain much more ICSRs which are at the same time distributed more heterogeneously compared to what a marketing authorization holder is required and able to collect.

The proposed standard package already includes some reports that go beyond the pure comparison of the DECs signal score as they cover comparable drugs, comparable events and also analyses on population subsets or potential interactions. This information however needs to be reviewed and evaluated by a medicinal product expert in order to interpret the data in the light of the event's or product's nature. Interpretation of such data in general needs to consider the limitations of both – the spontaneous databases and the statistical methods that are applied.

The implementation of processes to use the external databases during the signal investigation period will help to gather more experience with the interpretation of the results and might lead to a more information based decision making. Also, retrospective analyses of data as done in the PROTECT project[78] will show which external databases and which algorithms should best be used for signal detection purposes. This will potentially increase patient safety by identifying drug safety signals earlier than today.

---

[78] PROTECT (2011), 2.

Bibliographic References

Lindquist M. (2008).
VigiBase, the WHO Global ICSR Database System: Basic Facts.
In: Drug Information Journal, 2008 (42).

CIOMS Working Group VIII (2010).
Practical Aspects of Signal Detection in Pharmacovigilance.

European Commission (2008).
Volume 9A - Pharmacovigilance for Medicinal Products for Human Use.

Rosati (2009).
Using electronic health information for pharmacovigilance: the promise and the pitfalls
In: J Health Life Sci Law. 2009 Jul;2(4):171.

Meyboom et al.(1997).
Principles of signal detection in pharmacovigilance
In: Drug Safety (1997):16(6).

United States Food and Drug Administration (2005).
U.S. Department of Health and Human Services
Guidance for Industry (March 2005) –
Good Pharmacovigilance Practices and Pharmacoepidemiologic Assessment.

United States Food and Drug Administration (2008), 1.
Department of Health and Human Services
New Molecular Entity Review Follow-up.

United States Food and Drug Administration (2008), 2.
Specifications for Preparing and Submitting Electronic ICSRs and ICSR Attachments.

Manfred Hauben, Lester Reich (2005).
Communication of findings in pharmacovigilance: use of the term "signal" and the need for precision in use
In: Eur J Clin Pharmacol (2005) 61.

Egberts (2007).
Signal Detection Historical Background
In: Drug Safety (2007): 30(7).

van Manen, Fram, DuMouchel (2007).
Signal detection methodologies to support effective safety management.
In: Expert Opinion on Drug Safety (2007): 6(4).

Napke (1968).
Drug adverse reaction alerting program
In: Canadian family physician (1968): 14(5).

Evans, Waller, Davis (2001).
Use of proportional reporting ratios (PRR) for signal generation from spontanous adverse drug reaction reports
In: Pharmacoepidemiology and drug safety (2001): 10(6).

Begaud (2000).
Dictionary Of Pharmacoepidemiology,
John Wiley & Sons; 1st circulation (28. September 2000).

Bate, Evans (2009).
Quantitative signal detection using spontaneous ADR reporting
In: Pharmacoepidemiology and drug safety (2009): 18(6).

Fitzmartin, Wise (2010).
Pharmacovigilance in the 'New Pharma'
In: Drug Development (2010):5.

Alvarez, et al. (2010).

Validation of Statistical Signal Detection Procedures in EudraVigilance Post-Authorization Data

A Retrospective Evaluation of the Potential for Earlier Signalling

In: Drug safety (2010): 33(6).

Marshal, Beevers (1996).

Alpha-adrenoceptor blocking drugs and female urinary incontinence: prevalence and reversibility.

In: British Journal of Clinical Pharmacology (1996): 42(4).

Hauben (2007).

Detection of spironolactone-associated hyperkalaemia following the Randomized Aldactone Evaluation Study (RALES).

In: Drug Safety (2007): 30(12).

Hapani, Chu, Wu (2009).

Risk of gastrointestinal perforation in patients with cancer treated with bevacizumab: a meta-analysis.

In: The lancet oncology (June 2009): 10(6).

Greil, Micksche (2006).

Arzneimittelprofil Sorafenib

In: ArzneimittelPROFIL Onkologie (Dezember 2006).

Gupta (2010).

Ensuring Patient Safety - Launching the New Pharmacovigilance Programme of India.

In: Pharma Times (2010): 42(8).

World Health Organization (2002).

Safety of medicines: A guide to detecting and reporting adverse drug reactions.

In: WHO/EDM/QSM (2002): 2.

Internet References

United States Food and Drug Administration (2011), 1.
URL: *http://www.fda.gov/Safety/FDAsSentinelInitiative/*.
Accessed:2011-05-03 (Archived by WebCite® at
www.webcitation.org/5yP8GTJ30)

United States Food and Drug Administration (2011), 2.
URL:*http://www.fda.gov/RegulatoryInformation/foi/default.htm*.
Accessed: 2011-07-10 (Archived by WebCite® at
http://www.webcitation.org/604LoOR1B)

United States Food and Drug Administration (2011), 3.
URL:*http://www.fda.gov/Drugs/GuidanceComplianceRegulatoryInformation/Surveillance/AdverseDrugEffects/ucm082193.htm*.
Accessed: 2011-07-10. (Archived by WebCite® at
http://www.webcitation.org/604MRx4Ah)

United States Food and Drug Administration (2010).
URL:*http://www.fda.gov/Drugs/GuidanceComplianceRegulatoryInformation/Surveillance/AdverseDrugEffects/ucm070093.htm*.
Accessed: 2011-05-04 (Archived by WebCite® at
www.webcitation.org/5yQOmnlXB)

United States Food and Drug Administration (2009), 1.
URL:*http://www.fda.gov/BiologicsBloodVaccines/SafetyAvailability/ReportaProblem/VaccineAdverseEvents/QuestionsabouttheVaccineAdverseEventReportingSystemVAERS/default.htm*.
Accessed: 2011-07-10. (Archived by WebCite® at
http://www.webcitation.org/604YYDlCW)

United States Food and Drug Administration (2009), 2.
URL:http://www.fda.gov/Drugs/GuidanceComplianceRegulatoryInformation/Surveillance/AdverseDrugEffects/default.htm.
Accessed: 2011-07-17. (Archived by WebCite® at
http://www.webcitation.org/60FFLPoDo)

World Health Organization (2011), 1.
URL: *http://who-umc.org/DynPage.aspx?id=98082&mn1=7347&mn2=7252&mn3=7322&mn4=7326.*
Accessed: 2011-05-04 (Archived by WebCite® at www.webcitation.org/5yQPGb7NT)

World Health Organization (2011), 2.
URL:*http://www.umc-products.com/DynPage.aspx?id=73567&mn1=1107&mn2=1132&mn3=6052.*
Accessed: 2011-07-10. (Archived by WebCite® at http://www.webcitation.org/604bzkBiM)

European Medicines Agency (2011).
Important Medical Event List
URL: *http://www.meddramsso.com/files_acrobat/IME_List_Coding_indications_project.pdf*
Accessed: 2011-05-11 (Archived by WebCite® at http://www.webcitation.org/5yb44hpeg)

European Medicines Agency (2010).
URL:*http://www.ema.europa.eu/ema/index.jsp?curl=pages/news_and_events/news/2010/05/news_detail_001030.jsp&mid=WC0b01ac058004d5c1&murl=menus/news_and_events/news_and_events.jsp&jsenabled=true.* Accessed: 2011-05-11 (Archived by WebCite® at http://www.webcitation.org/5yb8UJPUZ)

Touraille (2010).
URL:*http://www.afssaps.fr/content/download/26717/354057/version/3/file/110610-cftgeudravigilance.pdf.*
Accessed: 2011-07-10. (Archived by WebCite® at http://www.webcitation.org/604oad39V)

United States Federal Business Opportunities (2010).
URL:*https://www.fbo.gov/index?s=opportunity&mode=form&id=15e3ef5d540a37972967de2a02f403d5&tab=core&_cview=1.*
Accessed:2011-05-11(Archived by WebCite® at http://www.webcitation.org/5yb8mHal2)

Medicines and Healthcare products Regulatory Agency (2010)
URL: *http://stats-www.open.ac.uk/SMOD/seabroke.pdf.*
Accessed: 2011-05-13. (Archived by WebCite® at http://www.webcitation.org/5yeOiTpfx)

Oracle (2010), 1.
URL: *http://www.oracle.com/us/corporate/press/068204.*
Accessed: 2011-05-14 (Archived by WebCite® at http://www.webcitation.org/5yfhUInaM)

Oracle (2010), 2.
URL:http://www.phaseforward.com/products/safety/stratpharma/default.aspx.

Accessed: 2011-05-14. (Archived by WebCite® at
http://www.webcitation.org/5yfi2m61Y)

PROTECT (2011), 1.
URL:http://www.imi-protect.eu/index.html. Accessed: 2011-05-14.
(Archived by WebCite® at http://www.webcitation.org/5yfnsgVS5)

PROTECT (2011), 2.
URL: *http://www.imi-protect.eu/wp3.html*.
Accessed: 2011-05-14. (Archived by WebCite® at
http://www.webcitation.org/5yfoJaI6E)

Investor Daily (2006).
URL:http://www.investordaily.com/cps/rde/xchg/id/style/801.htm?rdeCOQ=SID-3F579BCE-819F182C.
Accessed: 2011-07-10. (Archived by WebCite® at
http://www.webcitation.org/604mSWCDT)

European Commission (2011).
URL: http://ec.europa.eu/health/documents/community-register/html/h342.htm.
Accessed: 2011-05-14. (Archived by WebCite® at
http://www.webcitation.org/5yfq7Fh38)

Bayer Pharma AG (2011).
URL:http://www.bayerpharma.de/de/unternehmen/ueber_uns/top_10_produkte/index.php.
Accessed: 2011-05-14. (Archived by WebCite® at
http://www.webcitation.org/5yfqiMtuc)

U.S. National Library of Medicine – MedlinePlus (2010).
URL:http://www.nlm.nih.gov/medlineplus/ency/article/000235.htm.
Accessed: 2011-05-14. (Archived by WebCite® at
http://www.webcitation.org/5yfsjEdHv)

Norwegian Institute of Public Health (2011), 1.
URL:http://www.fhi.no/eway/default.aspx?pid=238&trg=MainLeft_5976&MainArea_5
811=5976:0:15,5012:1:0:0:::0:0&MainLeft_5976=5825:87991::1:5977:14:::0:0.
Accessed: 2011-06-03. (Archived by WebCite® at
http://www.webcitation.org/5zA1kxbly)

Norwegian Institute of Public Health (2011), 2.
URL:http://www.whocc.no/atc/structure_and_principles/.
Accessed: 2011-07-17. (Archived by WebCite® at
http://www.webcitation.org/60F6fqKXR)

Norwegian Institute of Public Health (2011), 3.
URL:http://www.whocc.no/atc_ddd_index/?code=L01XE05&showdescription=yes. Accessed: 2011-07-17. (Archived by WebCite® at
http://www.webcitation.org/60F70xWKc)

Norwegian Institute of Public Health (2010), 1.
URL:http://www.whocc.no/atc_ddd_index/?code=N02BA01&showdescription =yes. Accessed: 2011-07-17. (Archived by WebCite® at http://www.webcitation.org/60F775599)

Norwegian Institute of Public Health (2010), 2.
URL:*http://www.whocc.no/atc_ddd_index/?code=B01AC06&showdescription=yes*. Accessed: 2011-07-17. (Archived by WebCite® at http://www.webcitation.org/60F7DZqzv)

Wikimedia Foundation (2008).
URL:*http://de.wikibooks.org/wiki/Pharmakologie_und_Toxikologie:_Wechsel-_und_Nebenwirkungen.*
Accessed: 2011-07-17. (Archived by WebCite® at http://www.webcitation.org/60F9eobzE)

MedDRA MSSO (2011), 1.
URL:*http://www.meddramsso.com/.*
Accessed: 2011-07-17. (Archived by WebCite® at http://www.webcitation.org/60F7K9UB0)

MedDRA MSSO (2011), 2.
URL:*http://www.meddramsso.com/subscriber_smq.asp.*
Accessed: 2011-07-17. (Archived by WebCite® at http://www.webcitation.org/60F7opAV5)

Penn State Lehigh Valley University (2010).
URL:http://www2.lv.psu.edu/jxm57/irp/chisquar.html.
Accessed: 2011-07-17. (Archived by WebCite® at http://www.webcitation.org/60F84Djvs)

OMOP (2011),
URL:*http://omop.fnih.org/.*
Accessed: 2011-07-17. (Archived by WebCite® at http://www.webcitation.org/60FDlINJP)

Annexes

Annex I: Bayer Pharma MedDRA search intestinal perforation

adresse	http://by-gds.bayer-ag.com/gcmeddraprd/meddralite.home

Search Contains ⊙ Search Starts With ○ Search On Code ○ MTG name contains ○
Find a Term (((intestinal perforation [FIND] [RESET] BACK TO NORMAL FIND
And ○ Or ○) Search in LEVELS : LLT+SYN ⊙ LLT ○ ALL ○
And ○ Or ○) ☑ LLT+SYN Hierarchy ☐ Search current term only
And ○ Or ○)

```
⊞ SOC: Gastrointestinal disorders
  ⊞ HLGT: Gastrointestinal ulceration and perforation
    ⊟ HLT: Intestinal ulcers and perforation NEC
      ⊞ PT:  Appendicitis perforated
      ⊞ PT:  Ileal perforation
      ⊞ PT:  Ileal ulcer
      ⊞ PT:  Ileal ulcer perforation
      ⊟ PT:  Intestinal perforation
          ⊞ LLT:  Bowel perforation
          ⊞ LLT:  Intestinal perforation
            LLT:  Intestinal perforation NOS
            LLT (Inactive): Peforation bowel
            LLT:  Perforated bowel
            LLT:  Perforation bowel
          ⊞ LLT:  Perforation intestinal
            LLT:  Perforation of intestine
            LLT:  Perinatal intestinal perforation
      ⊞ PT:  Intestinal ulcer
      ⊞ PT:  Intestinal ulcer perforation
      ⊞ PT:  Jejunal perforation
      ⊞ PT:  Jejunal ulcer
      ⊞ PT:  Jejunal ulcer perforation
      ⊞ PT:  Large intestinal ulcer
      ⊞ PT:  Large intestinal ulcer haemorrhage
      ⊞ PT:  Large intestine perforation
      ⊞ PT:  Small intestinal perforation
      ⊞ PT:  Small intestinal ulcer haemorrhage
      ⊞ PT:  Small intestine ulcer
```

Details:

Level	Preferred Term
Term	Intestinal perforation
Code	10022694
Hyperlink	Google search

Annex II: Bar Graph Drug and Events EBGM VigiBase Q1 2011

Empirica Outputs\ Bar Graph drug and even

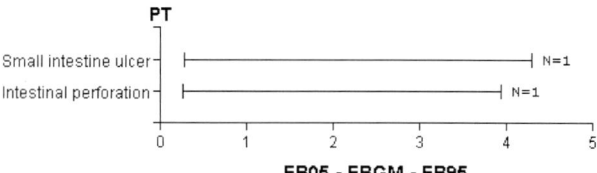

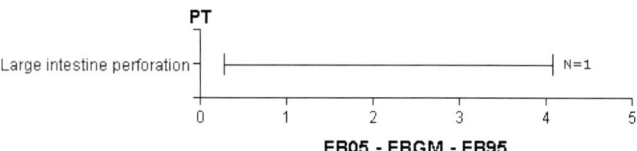

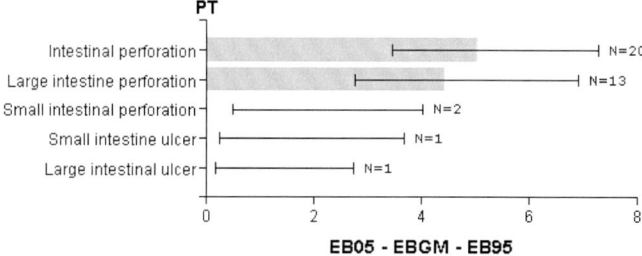

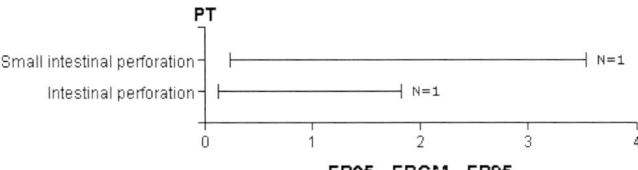

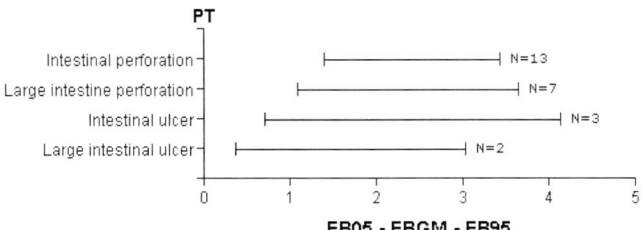

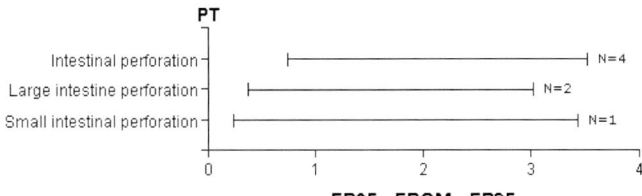

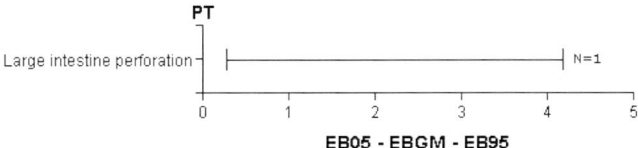

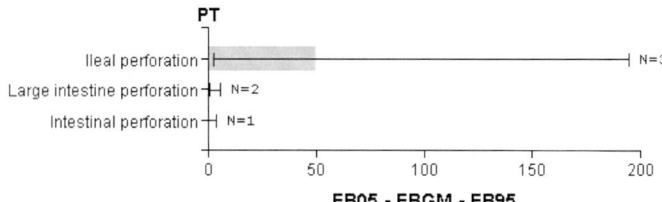

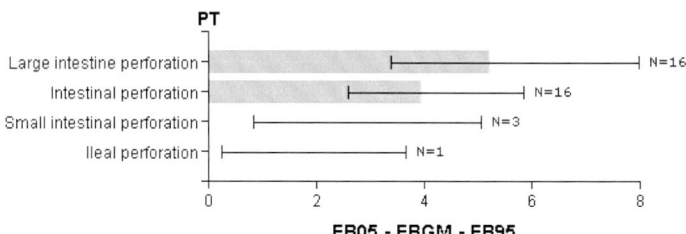

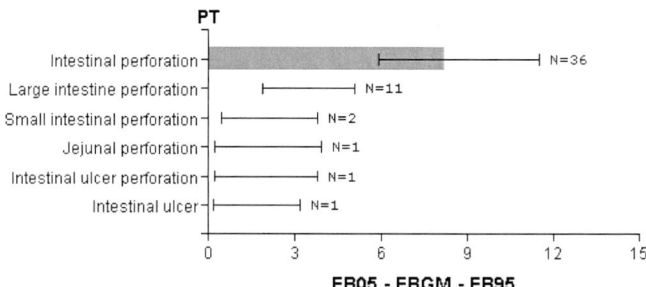

Notes

Run
- Name: 2011Q1 Vigibase Generic (S)
- ID: 78
- Description: 2011Q1 Generic_Name (Abridged); Suspect and Interacting Drugs only; Minimum count=1; Standard strata (AgeGroup9, Data Mining Year, Gender); includes PRR and ROR; includes hierarchy information.
- Created By: Empirica Signal Administrator
- Created Date: 01-Apr-2011 04:11:24 CEST
- Configuration: 2011Q1: Vigibase (S)
- Drug Hierarchy: WHO-DD 2011Q1
- Event Hierarchy: MedDRA 13.1

Selection Criteria
- Dimension: 2
- Pattern: Generic_Name (Abridged)(ATC4=Protein Kinase Inhibitors) + PT(HLT=Intestinal ulcers and perforation NEC)

Display Options
- Bar color controlled by EB05
- Bars ordered by bar length

Annex III: Bar Graph SMQ PTs and Drugs with Credible Intervals EBGM FDA Q3 2010

Empirica Outputs\ Bar Graph SMQ PTs and

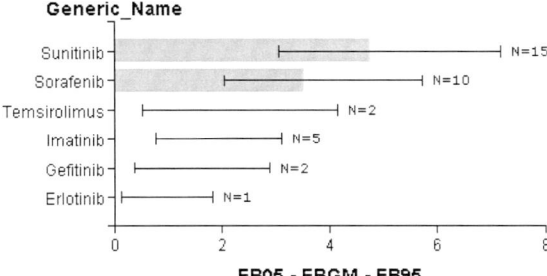
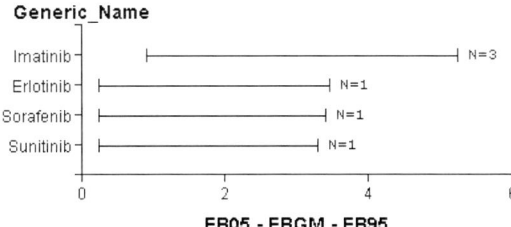
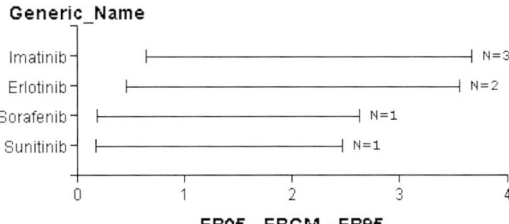
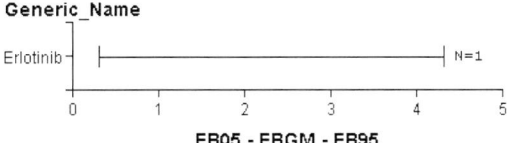

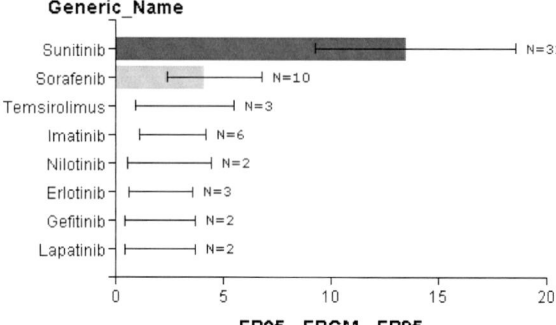

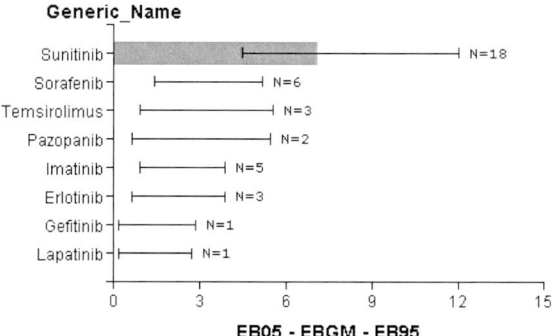

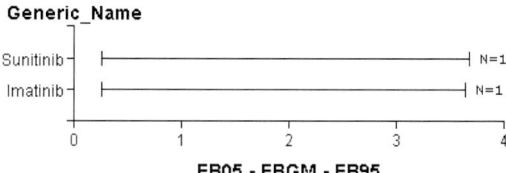

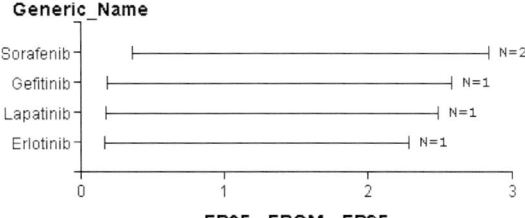

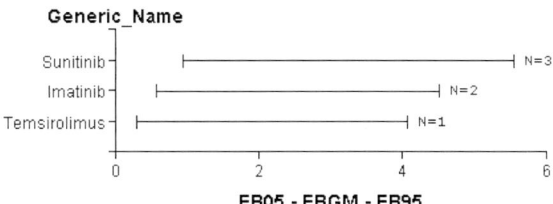

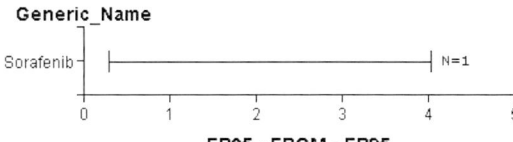

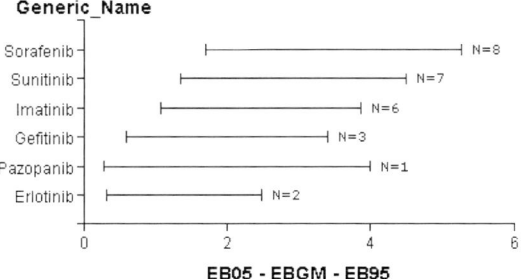

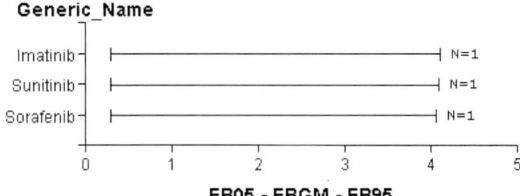

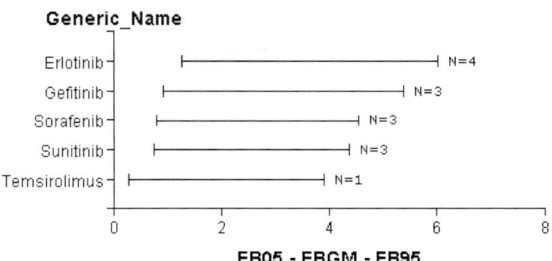

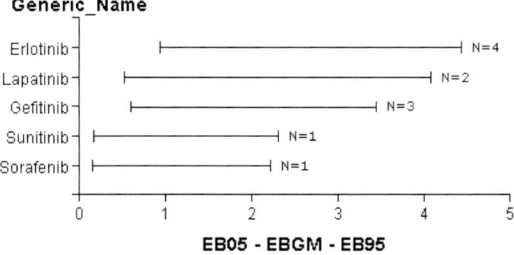

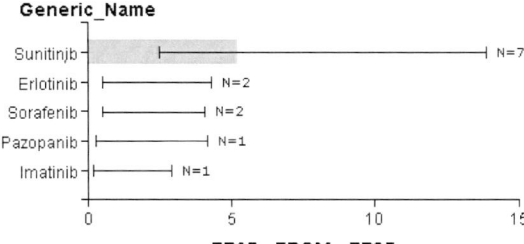

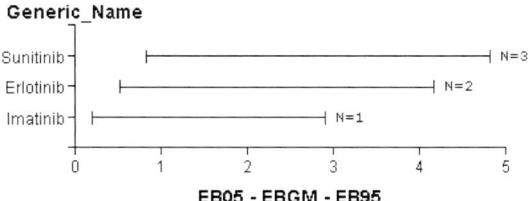

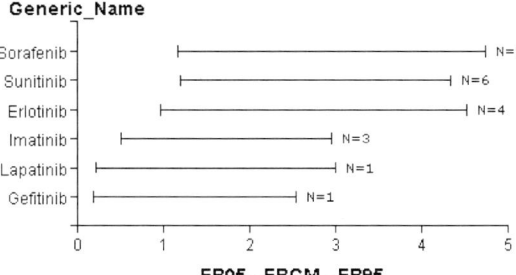

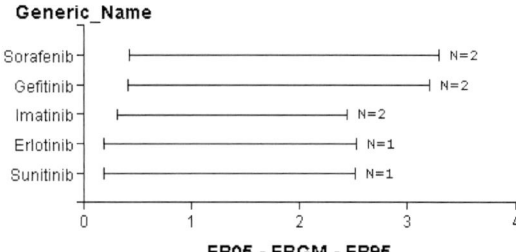

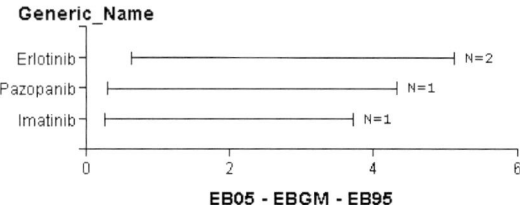

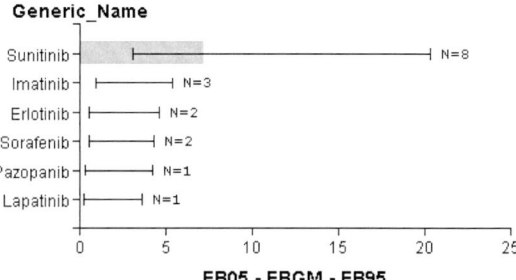

Event=Gastrointestinal perforation

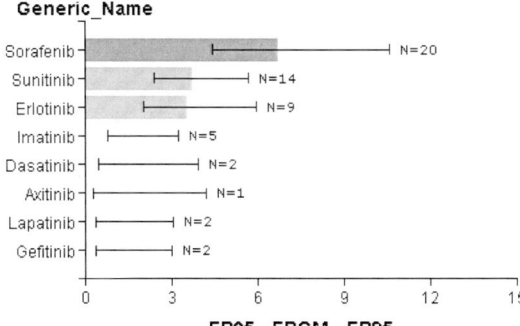

Event=Gastrointestinal ulcer perforation

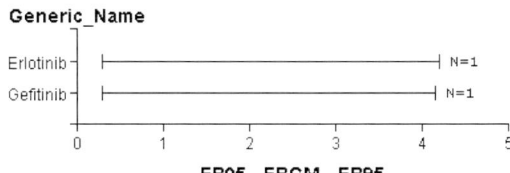

Event=Ileal perforation

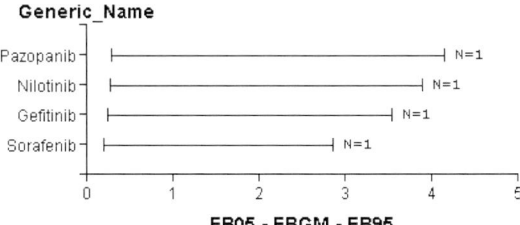

Event=Ileal ulcer perforation

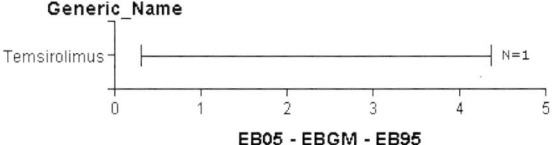

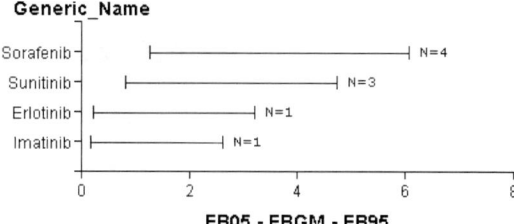

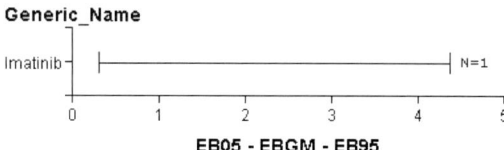

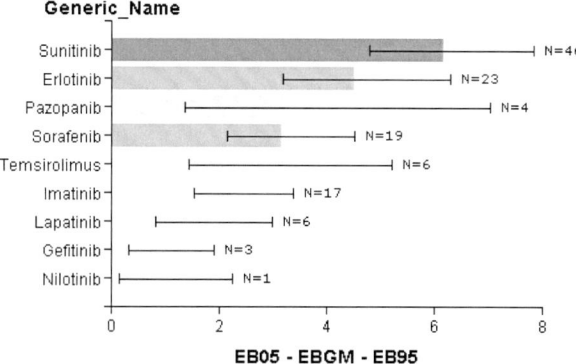

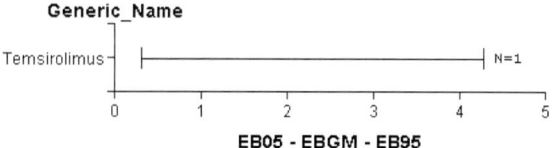

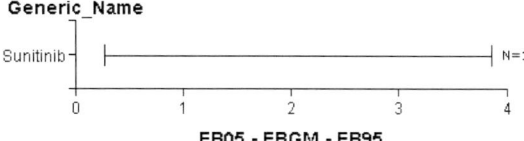

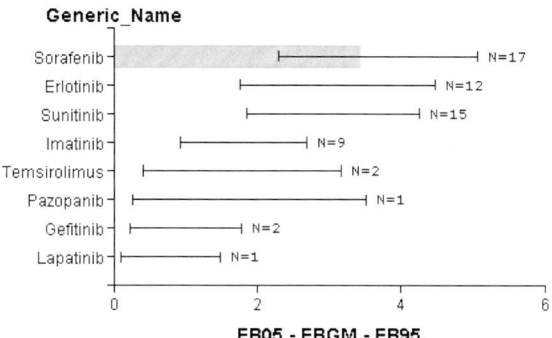

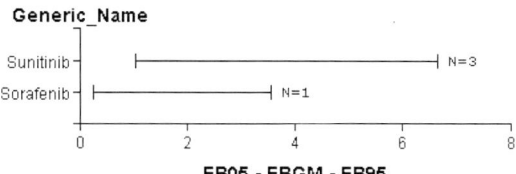

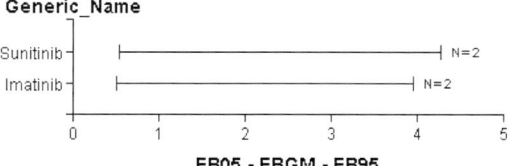

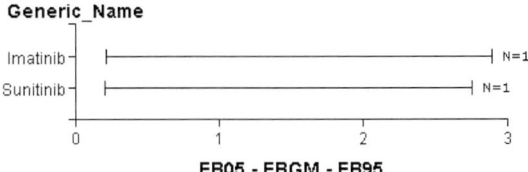

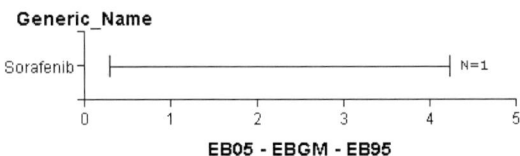

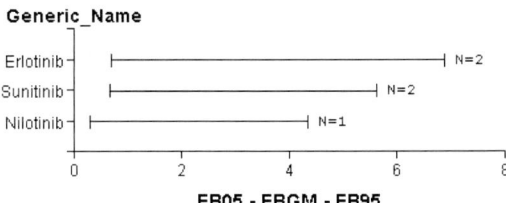

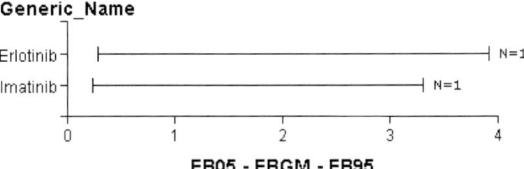

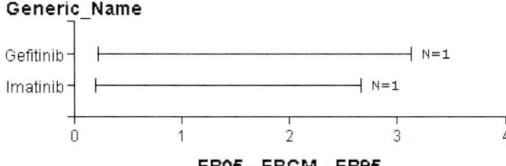

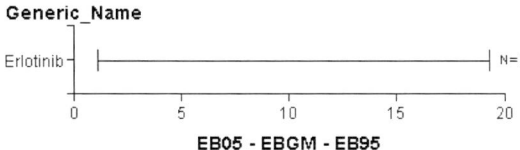

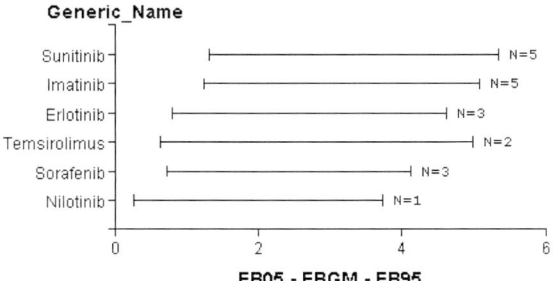

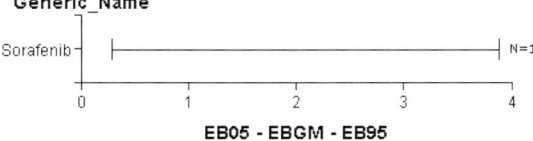

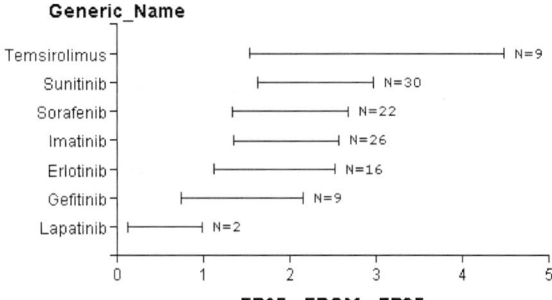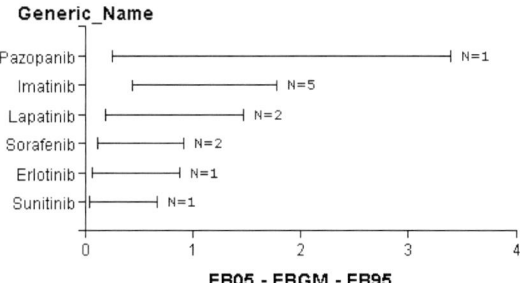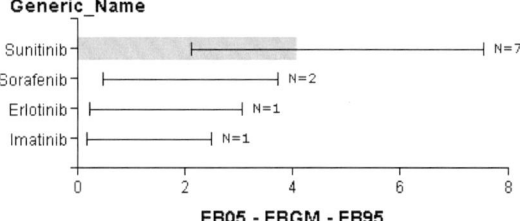

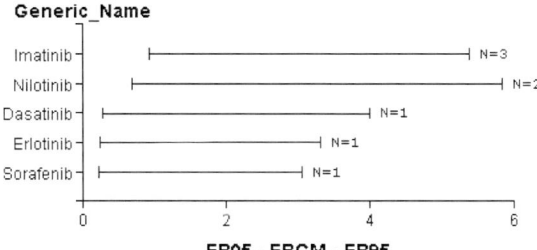

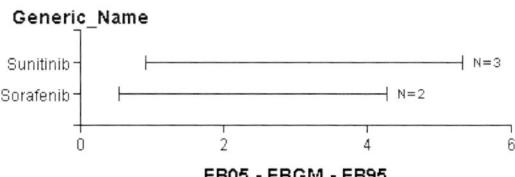

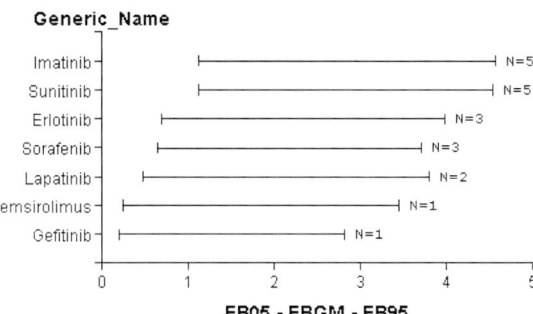

Notes

Run
- Name: 2010Q3 Generic (S)
- ID: 76
- Description: 2010Q3 Generic; Suspect Drugs only; Minimum count=1; Standard strata (Age, FDA_Year, Gender); includes unstratified PRR and ROR; includes hierarchy information.
- Created By: Empirica Signal Administrator
- Created Date: 23-Mar-2011 20:41:29 CET
- Configuration: 2010Q3: AERS+SRS (S)
- Drug Hierarchy: ATC 2010Q3
- Event Hierarchy: MedDRA 13.1

Selection Criteria
- Dimension: 2
- Pattern: Generic_Name(ATC4=Protein Kinase Inhibitors) + PT_plus_Narrow_Alg_SMQ(PT=...)

Display Options
- Bar color controlled by EB05
- Bars ordered by bar length

Annex IV: Map Graph ATC4 Drugs + SMQ EBGM by Subset Gender

Empirica Outputs\
MapGraph ATC4 drug

Event=Gastrointestinal perforation (SMQ) [narrow]

	F	Σ	U
Sunitinib	6.543	3.294	4.339
Pazopanib	5.277	1.361	
Sorafenib	3.483	2.604	4.537
Erlotinib	2.693	2.748	4.122
Temsirolimus	0.862	2.813	2.657
Imatinib	1.711	1.795	2.283
Gefitinib	1.342	0.993	0.879
Lapatinib	0.933	1.047	0.975
Axitinib		0.973	
Nilotinib	0.925	0.584	
Dasatinib	0.499	0.229	

0 ≤ EB05 ≤ 1 < EB05 ≤ 2 < EB05 ≤ 4 < EB05 ≤ 8 < EB05 < ∞

Notes

Run
  Name: FDA all Q3 2010 subset gender
  ID: 86
  Created By: Denny Lorenz
  Created Date: 18-May-2011 15:04:40 CEST
  Configuration: 2010Q3: AERS+SRS (S)
  Drug Hierarchy: ATC 2010Q3
  Event Hierarchy: MedDRA 13.1
Selection Criteria
  Dimension: 2
  Pattern: Generic_Name(ATC4=Protein Kinase Inhibitors) + PT_plus_Narrow_Alg_SMQ (PT=Gastrointestinal perforation (SMQ) [narrow])
  Subset: (All)
Display Options
  Show value of EBGM
  Color controlled by EB05
  Bars ordered by high value

Annex V: Map Graph ATC4 Drugs + SMQ EBGM by Subset Age Group

Empirica Outputs\
MapGraph ATC4 drug

Event=Gastrointestinal perforation (SMQ) [narrow]

	00_17	18_64	65_above	UNK
Sunitinib		5.083	2.429	5.331
Sorafenib		3.773	2.08	2.89
Everolimus		1.846	1.481	3.732
Erlotinib		3.708	1.883	3.064
Pazopanib		3.408	2.62	
Temsirolimus		2.161	2.152	2.8
Imatinib	1.263	1.641	2.096	1.404
Gefitinib		1.08	1.284	0.589
Nilotinib		1.244	0.385	
Axitinib		1.095		
Lapatinib		0.998	0.852	1.057
Dasatinib		0.271	0.537	

$0 \leq EB05 \leq 1 < EB05 \leq 2 < EB05 \leq 4 < EB05 \leq 8 < EB05 < \infty$

Notes

Run
- Name: FDA all Q3 2010 subset by age group 4
- ID: 87
- Created By: Denny Lorenz
- Created Date: 18-May-2011 15:06:06 CEST
- Configuration: 2010Q3: AERS+SRS (S)
- Drug Hierarchy: ATC 2010Q3
- Event Hierarchy: MedDRA 13.1

Selection Criteria
- Dimension: 2
- Pattern: Generic_Name(ATC5=...) + PT_plus_Narrow_Alg_SMQ(PT=Gastrointestinal perforation (SMQ) [narrow])
- Subset: (All)

Display Options
- Show value of EBGM
- Color controlled by EB05
- Bars ordered by high value

Annex VI: Nested Credible Interval Graph per Drug 3D

Empirica Outputs\
nested confidence int

Drug=Erlotinib

EB05-EBGM-EB95

Drug+Everolimus+Gastrointestinal perforation (S...	N=5
Drug+Gastrointestinal perforation (SMQ) [narrow]	N=99
Everolimus+Gastrointestinal perforation (SMQ) [...	N=37
Drug+Gemcitabine+Gastrointestinal perforation (...	N=15
Drug+Gastrointestinal perforation (SMQ) [narrow]	N=99
Gemcitabine+Gastrointestinal perforation (SMQ) ...	N=208
Drug+Fluorouracil+Gastrointestinal perforation ...	N=5
Drug+Gastrointestinal perforation (SMQ) [narrow]	N=99
Fluorouracil+Gastrointestinal perforation (SMQ)...	N=405
Drug+Carboplatin+Gastrointestinal perforation (...	N=5
Carboplatin+Gastrointestinal perforation (SMQ) ...	N=246
Drug+Gastrointestinal perforation (SMQ) [narrow]	N=99
Drug+Bevacizumab+Gastrointestinal perforation (...	N=42
Bevacizumab+Gastrointestinal perforation (SMQ) ...	N=913
Drug+Gastrointestinal perforation (SMQ) [narrow]	N=99

0   10

Drug=Lapatinib

EB05-EBGM-EB95

Drug+Trastuzumab+Gastrointestinal perforation (... ⊢————————⊣ N=5
Drug+Gastrointestinal perforation (SMQ) [narrow] ⊢——⊣ N=22
Trastuzumab+Gastrointestinal perforation (SMQ) ... ⊢————⊣ N=53

0   1   2   3   4   5

Drug=Sorafenib

EB05-EBGM-EB95

Drug+Gemcitabine+Gastrointestinal perforation (... ⊢————————⊣ N=8
Gemcitabine+Gastrointestinal perforation (SMQ) ... ⊢⊣ N=208
Drug+Gastrointestinal perforation (SMQ) [narrow] ⊢⊣ N=127

Drug+Cisplatin+Gastrointestinal perforation (SM... ⊢————————⊣ N=5
Cisplatin+Gastrointestinal perforation (SMQ) [n... ⊢⊣ N=294
Drug+Gastrointestinal perforation (SMQ) [narrow] ⊢⊣ N=127

Drug+Paclitaxel+Gastrointestinal perforation (S... ⊢————————⊣ N=5
Paclitaxel+Gastrointestinal perforation (SMQ) [... ⊢⊣ N=301
Drug+Gastrointestinal perforation (SMQ) [narrow] ⊢⊣ N=127

Drug+Bevacizumab+Gastrointestinal perforation (... ⊢——————————————————⊣ N=5
Bevacizumab+Gastrointestinal perforation (SMQ) ... ⊢⊣ N=913
Drug+Gastrointestinal perforation (SMQ) [narrow] ⊢⊣ N=127

0　　　　　　　　10

Drug=Sunitinib

EB05-EBGM-EB95

Drug+Fluorouracil+Gastrointestinal perforation ...	⊢————————————⊣ N=7
Fluorouracil+Gastrointestinal perforation (SMQ)...	⊢—⊣ N=405
Drug+Gastrointestinal perforation (SMQ) [narrow]	⊢—⊣ N=218
Drug+Irinotecan+Gastrointestinal perforation (S...	⊢————————————⊣ N=7
Irinotecan+Gastrointestinal perforation (SMQ) [...	⊢—⊣ N=229
Drug+Gastrointestinal perforation (SMQ) [narrow]	⊢—⊣ N=218
Drug+Folinic Acid+Gastrointestinal perforation ...	⊢————————————⊣ N=7
Folinic Acid+Gastrointestinal perforation (SMQ)...	⊢—⊣ N=235
Drug+Gastrointestinal perforation (SMQ) [narrow]	⊢—⊣ N=218

0   10

Drug=Temsirolimus

EB05-EBGM-EB95

Drug+Bevacizumab+Gastrointestinal perforation (... ⊢————⊣ N=15
Bevacizumab+Gastrointestinal perforation (SMQ) ... ⊢—⊣ N=913
Drug+Gastrointestinal perforation (SMQ) [narrow] ⊢——⊣ N=28

0   10

——— Confidence Interval where INTSS > 1.0
——— Confidence Interval where INTSS <= 1.0

Notes

Run
  Name: FDA all Q3 2010 3D with SMQ - 5 results
  ID: 94
  Description: min 5 results
  Created By: Denny Lorenz
  Created Date: 24-May-2011 09:55:30 CEST
  Configuration: 2010Q3: AERS+SRS (S)
  Drug Hierarchy: ATC 2010Q3
  Event Hierarchy: MedDRA 13.1
Selection Criteria
  Dimension: 3
  Pattern: Generic_Name(ATC4=Protein Kinase Inhibitors) + Any Generic_Name(ATC4) + PT_plus_Narrow_Alg_SMQ(PT=Gastrointestinal perforation (SMQ) [narrow])
Display Options
  Order by INTSS
  Axis type: linear

Annex VII: Nested Credible Interval Graph per Drug 3D with Suspect and Concomitant Products

Empirica Outputs\
nested confidence int

Drug=Erlotinib

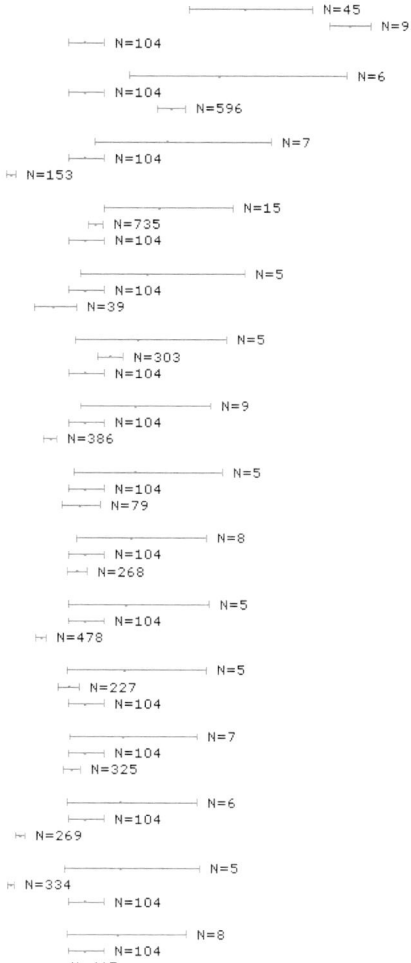

Drug=Erlotinib

EB05-EBGM-EB95

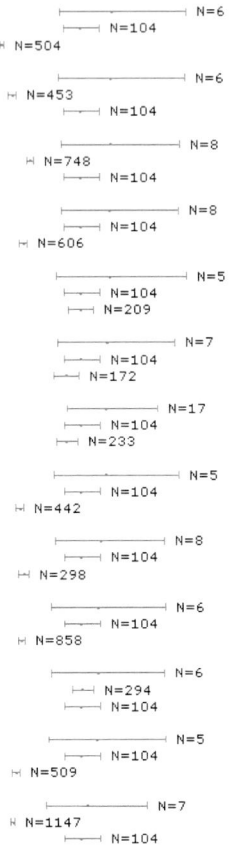

Drug+Levothyroxine+Gastrointestinal perforation...	N=6
Drug+Gastrointestinal perforation (SMQ) [narrow]	N=104
Levothyroxine+Gastrointestinal perforation (SMQ...	N=504
Drug+Amlodipine+Gastrointestinal perforation (S...	N=6
Amlodipine+Gastrointestinal perforation (SMQ) [...	N=453
Drug+Gastrointestinal perforation (SMQ) [narrow]	N=104
Drug+Acetaminophen+Gastrointestinal perforation...	N=8
Acetaminophen+Gastrointestinal perforation (SMQ...	N=748
Drug+Gastrointestinal perforation (SMQ) [narrow]	N=104
Drug+Omeprazole+Gastrointestinal perforation (S...	N=8
Drug+Gastrointestinal perforation (SMQ) [narrow]	N=104
Omeprazole+Gastrointestinal perforation (SMQ) [...	N=606
Drug+Sennoside+Gastrointestinal perforation (SM...	N=5
Drug+Gastrointestinal perforation (SMQ) [narrow]	N=104
Sennoside+Gastrointestinal perforation (SMQ) [n...	N=209
Drug+Prochlorperazine+Gastrointestinal perforat...	N=7
Drug+Gastrointestinal perforation (SMQ) [narrow]	N=104
Prochlorperazine+Gastrointestinal perforation (...	N=172
Drug+Gemcitabine+Gastrointestinal perforation (...	N=17
Drug+Gastrointestinal perforation (SMQ) [narrow]	N=104
Gemcitabine+Gastrointestinal perforation (SMQ) ...	N=233
Drug+Metoprolol+Gastrointestinal perforation (S...	N=5
Drug+Gastrointestinal perforation (SMQ) [narrow]	N=104
Metoprolol+Gastrointestinal perforation (SMQ) [...	N=442
Drug+Oxycodone+Gastrointestinal perforation (SM...	N=8
Drug+Gastrointestinal perforation (SMQ) [narrow]	N=104
Oxycodone+Gastrointestinal perforation (SMQ) [n...	N=298
Drug+Furosemide+Gastrointestinal perforation (S...	N=6
Drug+Gastrointestinal perforation (SMQ) [narrow]	N=104
Furosemide+Gastrointestinal perforation (SMQ) [...	N=858
Drug+Carboplatin+Gastrointestinal perforation (...	N=6
Carboplatin+Gastrointestinal perforation (SMQ) ...	N=294
Drug+Gastrointestinal perforation (SMQ) [narrow]	N=104
Drug+Vitamin+Gastrointestinal perforation (SMQ)...	N=5
Drug+Gastrointestinal perforation (SMQ) [narrow]	N=104
Vitamin+Gastrointestinal perforation (SMQ) [nar...	N=509
Drug+Aspirin+Gastrointestinal perforation (SMQ)...	N=7
Aspirin+Gastrointestinal perforation (SMQ) [nar...	N=1147
Drug+Gastrointestinal perforation (SMQ) [narrow]	N=104

0   10

Drug=Gefitinib

EB05-EBGM-EB95

Drug+Radiation Therapy-V...+Gastrointestinal pe...   N=6
Drug+Gastrointestinal perforation (SMQ) [narrow]   N=27
Radiation Therapy-Ver...+Gastrointestinal perfo...   N=124

Drug+Unmapped+Gastrointestinal perforation (SMQ...   N=5
Drug+Gastrointestinal perforation (SMQ) [narrow]   N=27
Unmapped+Gastrointestinal perforation (SMQ) [na...   N=923

0   1   2   3   4

Drug=Imatinib

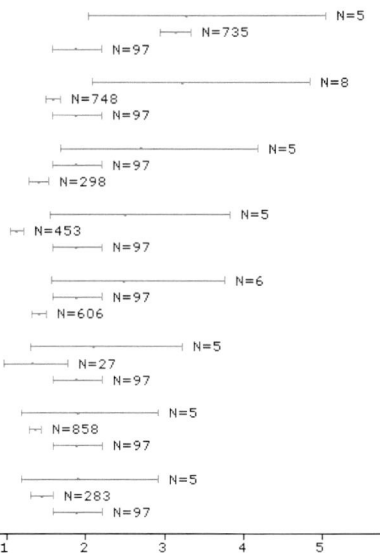

Drug=Lapatinib

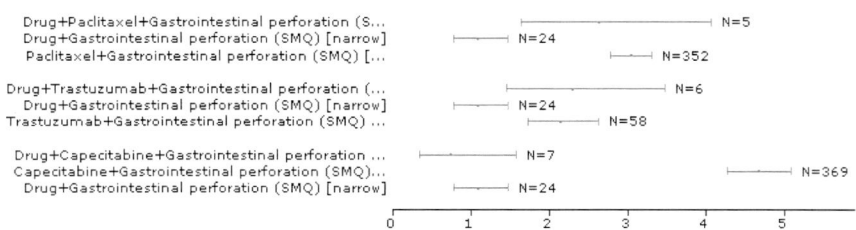

Drug=Sorafenib

EB05-EBGM-EB95

Drug+Bevacizumab+Gastrointestinal perforation (...	N=6
Bevacizumab+Gastrointestinal perforation (SMQ) ...	N=939
Drug+Gastrointestinal perforation (SMQ) [narrow]	N=131
Drug+Dexamethasone+Gastrointestinal perforation...	N=21
Dexamethasone+Gastrointestinal perforation (SMQ...	N=735
Drug+Gastrointestinal perforation (SMQ) [narrow]	N=131
Drug+Diclofenac+Gastrointestinal perforation (S...	N=5
Diclofenac+Gastrointestinal perforation (SMQ) [...	N=577
Drug+Gastrointestinal perforation (SMQ) [narrow]	N=131
Drug+Potassium Chloride+Gastrointestinal perfor...	N=9
Potassium Chloride+Gastrointestinal perforation...	N=362
Drug+Gastrointestinal perforation (SMQ) [narrow]	N=131
Drug+Gemcitabine+Gastrointestinal perforation (...	N=10
Gemcitabine+Gastrointestinal perforation (SMQ) ...	N=233
Drug+Gastrointestinal perforation (SMQ) [narrow]	N=131
Drug+Morphine+Gastrointestinal perforation (SMQ...	N=12
Morphine+Gastrointestinal perforation (SMQ) [na...	N=415
Drug+Gastrointestinal perforation (SMQ) [narrow]	N=131
Drug+Diphenhydramine+Gastrointestinal perforati...	N=6
Diphenhydramine+Gastrointestinal perforation (S...	N=157
Drug+Gastrointestinal perforation (SMQ) [narrow]	N=131
Drug+Prednisone+Gastrointestinal perforation (S...	N=7
Prednisone+Gastrointestinal perforation (SMQ) [...	N=1042
Drug+Gastrointestinal perforation (SMQ) [narrow]	N=131
Drug+Prednisolone+Gastrointestinal perforation ...	N=5
Prednisolone+Gastrointestinal perforation (SMQ)...	N=685
Drug+Gastrointestinal perforation (SMQ) [narrow]	N=131
Drug+Oxycodone+Gastrointestinal perforation (SM...	N=15
Oxycodone+Gastrointestinal perforation (SMQ) [n...	N=298
Drug+Gastrointestinal perforation (SMQ) [narrow]	N=131
Drug+Hydrochlorothiazide+Gastrointestinal perfo...	N=7
Hydrochlorothiazide+Gastrointestinal perforatio...	N=185
Drug+Gastrointestinal perforation (SMQ) [narrow]	N=131
Drug+Ondansetron+Gastrointestinal perforation (...	N=8
Ondansetron+Gastrointestinal perforation (SMQ) ...	N=268
Drug+Gastrointestinal perforation (SMQ) [narrow]	N=131
Drug+Paclitaxel+Gastrointestinal perforation (S...	N=6
Paclitaxel+Gastrointestinal perforation (SMQ) [...	N=352
Drug+Gastrointestinal perforation (SMQ) [narrow]	N=131
Drug+Candesartan+Gastrointestinal perforation (...	N=5
Candesartan+Gastrointestinal perforation (SMQ) ...	N=70
Drug+Gastrointestinal perforation (SMQ) [narrow]	N=131
Drug+Enalapril+Gastrointestinal perforation (SM...	N=5
Enalapril+Gastrointestinal perforation (SMQ) [n...	N=179
Drug+Gastrointestinal perforation (SMQ) [narrow]	N=131

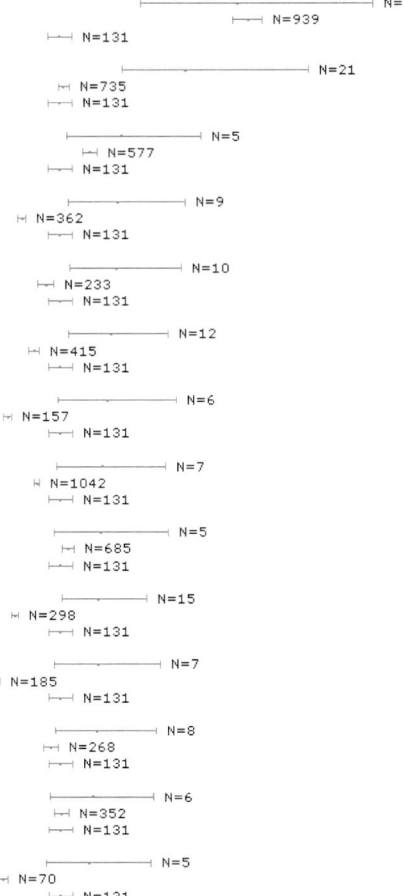

Drug=Sorafenib

EB05-EBGM-EB95

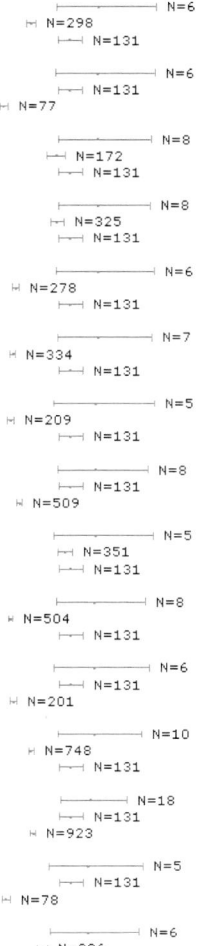

Drug+Acetaminophen And H...+Gastrointestinal pe...	N=6
Acetaminophen And Hyd...+Gastrointestinal perfo...	N=298
Drug+Gastrointestinal perforation (SMQ) [narrow]	N=131
Drug+Tamsulosin+Gastrointestinal perforation (S...	N=6
Drug+Gastrointestinal perforation (SMQ) [narrow]	N=131
Tamsulosin+Gastrointestinal perforation (SMQ) [...	N=77
Drug+Prochlorperazine+Gastrointestinal perforat...	N=8
Prochlorperazine+Gastrointestinal perforation (...	N=172
Drug+Gastrointestinal perforation (SMQ) [narrow]	N=131
Drug+Metoclopramide+Gastrointestinal perforatio...	N=8
Metoclopramide+Gastrointestinal perforation (SM...	N=325
Drug+Gastrointestinal perforation (SMQ) [narrow]	N=131
Drug+Lorazepam+Gastrointestinal perforation (SM...	N=6
Lorazepam+Gastrointestinal perforation (SMQ) [n...	N=278
Drug+Gastrointestinal perforation (SMQ) [narrow]	N=131
Drug+Atenolol+Gastrointestinal perforation (SMQ...	N=7
Atenolol+Gastrointestinal perforation (SMQ) [na...	N=334
Drug+Gastrointestinal perforation (SMQ) [narrow]	N=131
Drug+Gabapentin+Gastrointestinal perforation (S...	N=5
Gabapentin+Gastrointestinal perforation (SMQ) [...	N=209
Drug+Gastrointestinal perforation (SMQ) [narrow]	N=131
Drug+Vitamin+Gastrointestinal perforation (SMQ)...	N=8
Drug+Gastrointestinal perforation (SMQ) [narrow]	N=131
Vitamin+Gastrointestinal perforation (SMQ) [nar...	N=509
Drug+Cisplatin+Gastrointestinal perforation (SM...	N=5
Cisplatin+Gastrointestinal perforation (SMQ) [n...	N=351
Drug+Gastrointestinal perforation (SMQ) [narrow]	N=131
Drug+Levothyroxine+Gastrointestinal perforation...	N=8
Levothyroxine+Gastrointestinal perforation (SMQ...	N=504
Drug+Gastrointestinal perforation (SMQ) [narrow]	N=131
Drug+Zolpidem+Gastrointestinal perforation (SMQ...	N=6
Drug+Gastrointestinal perforation (SMQ) [narrow]	N=131
Zolpidem+Gastrointestinal perforation (SMQ) [na...	N=201
Drug+Acetaminophen+Gastrointestinal perforation...	N=10
Acetaminophen+Gastrointestinal perforation (SMQ...	N=748
Drug+Gastrointestinal perforation (SMQ) [narrow]	N=131
Drug+Unmapped+Gastrointestinal perforation (SMQ...	N=18
Drug+Gastrointestinal perforation (SMQ) [narrow]	N=131
Unmapped+Gastrointestinal perforation (SMQ) [na...	N=923
Drug+Zoledronic Acid+Gastrointestinal perforati...	N=5
Drug+Gastrointestinal perforation (SMQ) [narrow]	N=131
Zoledronic Acid+Gastrointestinal perforation (S...	N=78
Drug+Pantoprazole+Gastrointestinal perforation ...	N=6
Pantoprazole+Gastrointestinal perforation (SMQ)...	N=386
Drug+Gastrointestinal perforation (SMQ) [narrow]	N=131

Drug=Sorafenib

EB05-EBGM-EB95

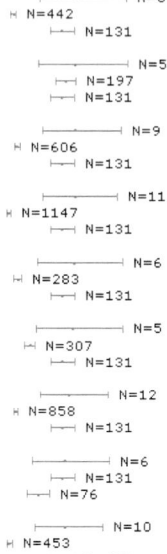

Drug+Metoprolol+Gastrointestinal perforation (S...	N=6
Metoprolol+Gastrointestinal perforation (SMQ) [...	N=442
Drug+Gastrointestinal perforation (SMQ) [narrow]	N=131
Drug+Loperamide+Gastrointestinal perforation (S...	N=5
Loperamide+Gastrointestinal perforation (SMQ) [...	N=197
Drug+Gastrointestinal perforation (SMQ) [narrow]	N=131
Drug+Omeprazole+Gastrointestinal perforation (S...	N=9
Omeprazole+Gastrointestinal perforation (SMQ) [...	N=606
Drug+Gastrointestinal perforation (SMQ) [narrow]	N=131
Drug+Aspirin+Gastrointestinal perforation (SMQ)...	N=11
Aspirin+Gastrointestinal perforation (SMQ) [nar...	N=1147
Drug+Gastrointestinal perforation (SMQ) [narrow]	N=131
Drug+Allopurinol+Gastrointestinal perforation (...	N=6
Allopurinol+Gastrointestinal perforation (SMQ) ...	N=283
Drug+Gastrointestinal perforation (SMQ) [narrow]	N=131
Drug+Famotidine+Gastrointestinal perforation (S...	N=5
Famotidine+Gastrointestinal perforation (SMQ) [...	N=307
Drug+Gastrointestinal perforation (SMQ) [narrow]	N=131
Drug+Furosemide+Gastrointestinal perforation (S...	N=12
Furosemide+Gastrointestinal perforation (SMQ) [...	N=858
Drug+Gastrointestinal perforation (SMQ) [narrow]	N=131
Drug+Ursodeoxycholic Acid+Gastrointestinal perf...	N=6
Drug+Gastrointestinal perforation (SMQ) [narrow]	N=131
Ursodeoxycholic Acid+Gastrointestinal perforati...	N=76
Drug+Amlodipine+Gastrointestinal perforation (S...	N=10
Amlodipine+Gastrointestinal perforation (SMQ) [...	N=453
Drug+Gastrointestinal perforation (SMQ) [narrow]	N=131

0   10

Drug=Sunitinib

EB05-EBGM-EB95

Drug+Acetaminophen And H...+Gastrointestinal pe...	⊢─┤ N=298	⊢──────────────┤ N=12
Acetaminophen And Hyd...+Gastrointestinal perfo...		⊢──┤ N=225
Drug+Gastrointestinal perforation (SMQ) [narrow]		
Drug+Folinic Acid+Gastrointestinal perforation ...		⊢─────────────┤ N=8
Folinic Acid+Gastrointestinal perforation (SMQ)...		⊢───┤ N=369
Drug+Gastrointestinal perforation (SMQ) [narrow]		⊢──┤ N=225
Drug+Sucralfate+Gastrointestinal perforation (S...		⊢──────────────┤ N=6
Sucralfate+Gastrointestinal perforation (SMQ) [...	⊢──┤ N=84	
Drug+Gastrointestinal perforation (SMQ) [narrow]		⊢──┤ N=225
Drug+Irinotecan+Gastrointestinal perforation (S...		⊢────────────┤ N=7
Irinotecan+Gastrointestinal perforation (SMQ) [...		⊢───┤ N=304
Drug+Gastrointestinal perforation (SMQ) [narrow]		⊢──┤ N=225
Drug+Fluorouracil+Gastrointestinal perforation ...		⊢─────────────┤ N=8
Fluorouracil+Gastrointestinal perforation (SMQ)...		⊢──┤ N=596
Drug+Gastrointestinal perforation (SMQ) [narrow]		⊢──┤ N=225
Drug+Lorazepam+Gastrointestinal perforation (SM...		⊢──────────────┤ N=12
Lorazepam+Gastrointestinal perforation (SMQ) [n...	⊢┤ N=278	
Drug+Gastrointestinal perforation (SMQ) [narrow]		⊢──┤ N=225
Drug+Levofloxacin+Gastrointestinal perforation ...		⊢─────────────┤ N=6
Levofloxacin+Gastrointestinal perforation (SMQ)...	⊢─┤ N=151	
Drug+Gastrointestinal perforation (SMQ) [narrow]		⊢──┤ N=225
Drug+Diclofenac+Gastrointestinal perforation (S...		⊢─────────────┤ N=9
Diclofenac+Gastrointestinal perforation (SMQ) [...		⊢─┤ N=577
Drug+Gastrointestinal perforation (SMQ) [narrow]		⊢──┤ N=225
Drug+Loperamide+Gastrointestinal perforation (S...		⊢──────────────┤ N=12
Loperamide+Gastrointestinal perforation (SMQ) [...		⊢──┤ N=197
Drug+Gastrointestinal perforation (SMQ) [narrow]		⊢──┤ N=225
Drug+Fentanyl+Gastrointestinal perforation (SMQ...		⊢──────────────┤ N=12
Fentanyl+Gastrointestinal perforation (SMQ) [na...	⊢┤ N=269	
Drug+Gastrointestinal perforation (SMQ) [narrow]		⊢──┤ N=225
Drug+Glyburide+Gastrointestinal perforation (SM...		⊢────────────┤ N=5
Glyburide+Gastrointestinal perforation (SMQ) [n...	⊢┤ N=97	
Drug+Gastrointestinal perforation (SMQ) [narrow]		⊢──┤ N=225
Drug+Levothyroxine+Gastrointestinal perforation...		⊢──────────┤ N=25
Levothyroxine+Gastrointestinal perforation (SMQ...	⊢┤ N=504	
Drug+Gastrointestinal perforation (SMQ) [narrow]		⊢──┤ N=225
Drug+Magnesium Oxide+Gastrointestinal perforati...		⊢────────────┤ N=9
Magnesium Oxide+Gastrointestinal perforation (S...		⊢──┤ N=162
Drug+Gastrointestinal perforation (SMQ) [narrow]		⊢──┤ N=225
Drug+Paclitaxel+Gastrointestinal perforation (S...		⊢────────────┤ N=5
Paclitaxel+Gastrointestinal perforation (SMQ) [...		⊢─┤ N=352
Drug+Gastrointestinal perforation (SMQ) [narrow]		⊢──┤ N=225
Drug+Ibuprofen+Gastrointestinal perforation (SM...		⊢────────────┤ N=7
Ibuprofen+Gastrointestinal perforation (SMQ) [n...	⊢┤ N=478	
Drug+Gastrointestinal perforation (SMQ) [narrow]		⊢──┤ N=225

Drug=Sunitinib

EB05-EBGM-EB95

Term	N (left)	EB05-EBGM-EB95 (N)
Drug+Potassium Chloride+Gastrointestinal perfor...		N=7
Potassium Chloride+Gastrointestinal perforation...	N=362	
Drug+Gastrointestinal perforation (SMQ) [narrow]		N=225
Drug+Lisinopril+Gastrointestinal perforation (S...		N=11
Lisinopril+Gastrointestinal perforation (SMQ) [...	N=311	
Drug+Gastrointestinal perforation (SMQ) [narrow]		N=225
Drug+Valsartan+Gastrointestinal perforation (SM...		N=6
Drug+Gastrointestinal perforation (SMQ) [narrow]		N=225
Valsartan+Gastrointestinal perforation (SMQ) [n...	N=153	
Drug+Acetaminophen+Gastrointestinal perforation...		N=17
Acetaminophen+Gastrointestinal perforation (SMQ...	N=748	
Drug+Gastrointestinal perforation (SMQ) [narrow]		N=225
Drug+Pantoprazole+Gastrointestinal perforation ...		N=12
Pantoprazole+Gastrointestinal perforation (SMQ)...	N=386	
Drug+Gastrointestinal perforation (SMQ) [narrow]		N=225
Drug+Dexamethasone+Gastrointestinal perforation...		N=13
Dexamethasone+Gastrointestinal perforation (SMQ...	N=735	
Drug+Gastrointestinal perforation (SMQ) [narrow]		N=225
Drug+Zoledronic Acid+Gastrointestinal perforati...		N=9
Drug+Gastrointestinal perforation (SMQ) [narrow]		N=225
Zoledronic Acid+Gastrointestinal perforation (S...	N=78	
Drug+Hydrochlorothiazide+Gastrointestinal perfo...		N=7
Hydrochlorothiazide+Gastrointestinal perforatio...	N=185	
Drug+Gastrointestinal perforation (SMQ) [narrow]		N=225
Drug+Morphine+Gastrointestinal perforation (SMQ...		N=12
Morphine+Gastrointestinal perforation (SMQ) [na...	N=415	
Drug+Gastrointestinal perforation (SMQ) [narrow]		N=225
Drug+Ondansetron+Gastrointestinal perforation (...		N=7
Ondansetron+Gastrointestinal perforation (SMQ) ...	N=268	
Drug+Gastrointestinal perforation (SMQ) [narrow]		N=225
Drug+Vitamin+Gastrointestinal perforation (SMQ)...		N=8
Drug+Gastrointestinal perforation (SMQ) [narrow]		N=225
Vitamin+Gastrointestinal perforation (SMQ) [nar...	N=509	
Drug+Oxycodone+Gastrointestinal perforation (SM...		N=13
Oxycodone+Gastrointestinal perforation (SMQ) [n...	N=298	
Drug+Gastrointestinal perforation (SMQ) [narrow]		N=225
Drug+Esomeprazole+Gastrointestinal perforation ...		N=8
Esomeprazole+Gastrointestinal perforation (SMQ)...	N=269	
Drug+Gastrointestinal perforation (SMQ) [narrow]		N=225
Drug+Sennoside+Gastrointestinal perforation (SM...		N=7
Sennoside+Gastrointestinal perforation (SMQ) [n...	N=209	
Drug+Gastrointestinal perforation (SMQ) [narrow]		N=225
Drug+Famotidine+Gastrointestinal perforation (S...		N=5
Famotidine+Gastrointestinal perforation (SMQ) [...	N=307	
Drug+Gastrointestinal perforation (SMQ) [narrow]		N=225

Drug=Sunitinib

EB05-EBGM-EB95

Interaction	N	Result
Drug+Prednisone+Gastrointestinal perforation (S...		N=5
Prednisone+Gastrointestinal perforation (SMQ) [...	N=1042	
Drug+Gastrointestinal perforation (SMQ) [narrow]		N=225
Drug+Allopurinol+Gastrointestinal perforation (...		N=9
Allopurinol+Gastrointestinal perforation (SMQ) ...	N=283	
Drug+Gastrointestinal perforation (SMQ) [narrow]		N=225
Drug+Omeprazole+Gastrointestinal perforation (S...		N=17
Omeprazole+Gastrointestinal perforation (SMQ) [...	N=606	
Drug+Gastrointestinal perforation (SMQ) [narrow]		N=225
Drug+Prochlorperazine+Gastrointestinal perforat...		N=8
Prochlorperazine+Gastrointestinal perforation (...	N=172	
Drug+Gastrointestinal perforation (SMQ) [narrow]		N=225
Drug+Atorvastatin+Gastrointestinal perforation ...		N=7
Atorvastatin+Gastrointestinal perforation (SMQ)...	N=372	
Drug+Gastrointestinal perforation (SMQ) [narrow]		N=225
Drug+Lansoprazole+Gastrointestinal perforation ...		N=7
Lansoprazole+Gastrointestinal perforation (SMQ)...	N=361	
Drug+Gastrointestinal perforation (SMQ) [narrow]		N=225
Drug+Atenolol+Gastrointestinal perforation (SMQ...		N=8
Atenolol+Gastrointestinal perforation (SMQ) [na...	N=334	
Drug+Gastrointestinal perforation (SMQ) [narrow]		N=225
Drug+Metformin+Gastrointestinal perforation (SM...		N=5
Metformin+Gastrointestinal perforation (SMQ) [n...	N=186	
Drug+Gastrointestinal perforation (SMQ) [narrow]		N=225
Drug+Unmapped+Gastrointestinal perforation (SMQ...		N=9
Drug+Gastrointestinal perforation (SMQ) [narrow]		N=225
Unmapped+Gastrointestinal perforation (SMQ) [na...	N=923	
Drug+Metoclopramide+Gastrointestinal perforatio...		N=9
Metoclopramide+Gastrointestinal perforation (SM...	N=325	
Drug+Gastrointestinal perforation (SMQ) [narrow]		N=225
Drug+Simvastatin+Gastrointestinal perforation (...		N=5
Simvastatin+Gastrointestinal perforation (SMQ) ...	N=325	
Drug+Gastrointestinal perforation (SMQ) [narrow]		N=225
Drug+Aspirin+Gastrointestinal perforation (SMQ)...		N=10
Aspirin+Gastrointestinal perforation (SMQ) [nar...	N=1147	
Drug+Gastrointestinal perforation (SMQ) [narrow]		N=225
Drug+Furosemide+Gastrointestinal perforation (S...		N=9
Furosemide+Gastrointestinal perforation (SMQ) [...	N=858	
Drug+Gastrointestinal perforation (SMQ) [narrow]		N=225
Drug+Amlodipine+Gastrointestinal perforation (S...		N=12
Amlodipine+Gastrointestinal perforation (SMQ) [...	N=453	
Drug+Gastrointestinal perforation (SMQ) [narrow]		N=225
Drug+Metoprolol+Gastrointestinal perforation (S...		N=5
Metoprolol+Gastrointestinal perforation (SMQ) [...	N=442	
Drug+Gastrointestinal perforation (SMQ) [narrow]		N=225

Drug=Sunitinib

EB05-EBGM-EB95

0   10

Drug=Temsirolimus

EB05-EBGM-EB95

Drug+Bevacizumab+Gastrointestinal perforation (... — N=19
Bevacizumab+Gastrointestinal perforation (SMQ) ... — N=939
Drug+Gastrointestinal perforation (SMQ) [narrow] — N=30

0   10

——— Confidence Interval where INTSS > 1.0
——— Confidence Interval where INTSS <= 1.0

Notes

Run
- Name: FDA all (S+C) 3D Q3 2010 with SMQs min 5
- ID: 99
- Created By: Denny Lorenz
- Created Date: 07-Jun-2011 16:00:51 CEST
- Configuration: 2010Q3: AERS+SRS (S + C)
- Drug Hierarchy: ATC 2010Q3
- Event Hierarchy: MedDRA 13.1

Selection Criteria
- Dimension: 3
- Pattern: Generic_Name(ATC4=Protein Kinase Inhibitors) + Any Generic_Name(ATC4) + PT_plus_Narrow_Alg_SMQ(PT=Gastrointestinal perforation (SMQ) [narrow])

Display Options
- Order by EBGM
- Axis type: linear

Annex VIII: Nested Credible Interval Graph per Event 3D

Empirica Outputs\
nested confidence int

Event=Gastrointestinal perforation (SMQ) [narrow]

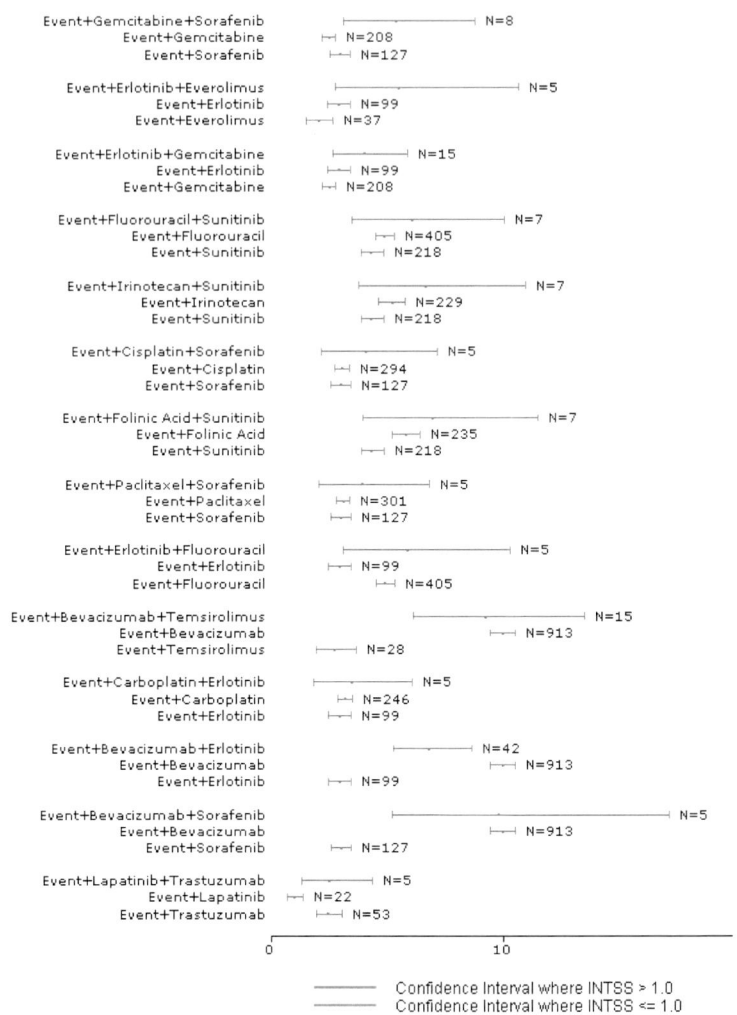

Notes

Run
- Name: FDA all Q3 2010 3D with SMQ - 5 results
- ID: 94
- Description: min 5 results
- Created By: Denny Lorenz
- Created Date: 24-May-2011 09:55:30 CEST
- Configuration: 2010Q3: AERS+SRS (S)
- Drug Hierarchy: ATC 2010Q3
- Event Hierarchy: MedDRA 13.1

Selection Criteria
- Dimension: 3
- Pattern: Generic_Name(ATC4=Protein Kinase Inhibitors) + Any Generic_Name(ATC4) + PT_plus_Narrow_Alg_SMQ(PT=Gastrointestinal perforation (SMQ) [narrow])

Display Options
- Order by INTSS
- Axis type: linear

SCHRIFTENREIHE MASTERSTUDIENGANG CONSUMER HEALTH CARE

herausgegeben von Prof. Dr. Marion Schaefer

ISSN 1869-6627

1 *Lena Harmann*
 Patienteninformation und Shared Decision Making im Lichte des
 Publikumswerbeverbotes für verschreibungspflichtige Arzneimittel
 ISBN 978-3-8382-0056-9

2 *Janna K. Schweim*
 Untersuchungen zum Arzneimittelversandhandel aus Verbrauchersicht
 ISBN 978-3-8382-0071-2

3 *Ansgar Muhle*
 Deutsche Gesundheitsportale im Netz
 Kritische Einschätzung anhand der gängigen Qualitätssiegel
 ISBN 978-3-8382-0086-6

4 *Elizabeth Storz*
 Psychopharmakamarkt in Deutschland
 Eine Untersuchung zu den Strukturveränderungen
 durch das Arzneiversorgungs-Wirtschaftlichkeitsgesetz (AVWG)
 ISBN 978-3-8382-0109-2

5 *Ursula Sellerberg*
 Heilpflanzen-Datenbanken im Internet
 Eine kritische Untersuchung anhand verbraucherrelevanter Kriterien
 ISBN 978-3-8382-0092-7

6 *Rüdiger Kolbeck*
 Arzneimittelfälschungen auf globaler und nationaler Ebene
 Eine Studie über das Problembewusstsein bei Patienten und Experten
 ISBN 978-3-8382-0155-9

7 *Silke Lauterbach*
 Das diabetische Fußsyndrom
 Ein Ratgeber zur Identifizierung von Risikopatienten in der Apotheke
 ISBN 978-3-8382-0182-5

8 *Judith Rommerskirchen*
 Die Arzneimittelrabattverträge der gesetzlichen Krankenversicherungen
 Eine Studie über Probleme bei ihrer Umsetzung an der Schnittstelle von Arzt und Apotheker
 ISBN 978-3-8382-0253-2

9   *Verena Purrucker*
    Möglichkeiten und Grenzen von Franchisesystemen in der zahnärztlichen
    Versorgung in Deutschland
    ISBN 978-3-8382-0186-3

10 *Stefan Prüller*
    Risiken und Nebenwirkungen auf der Spur
    Konsumentenberichte über unerwünschte Arzneimittelwirkungen als Chance für
    Krankenkassen
    ISBN 978-3-8382-0318-8

11 *Denny Lorenz*
    Development of a Standard Report for Signal Verification on Public Adverse
    Event Databases
    ISBN 978-3-8382-0432-1

Abonnement

Hiermit abonniere ich die **Schriftenreihe Masterstudiengang Consumer Health Care (ISSN 1869-6627),** herausgegeben von Prof. Dr. Marion Schaefer,

❐ ab Band # 1
❐ ab Band # ___
  ❐ Außerdem bestelle ich folgende der bereits erschienenen Bände:
     #___, ___, ___, ___, ___, ___, ___, ___, ___, ___, ___, ___

❐ ab der nächsten Neuerscheinung
  ❐ Außerdem bestelle ich folgende der bereits erschienenen Bände:
     #___, ___, ___, ___, ___, ___, ___, ___, ___, ___, ___, ___

❐ 1 Ausgabe pro Band   ODER   ❐ ___ Ausgaben pro Band

Bitte senden Sie meine Bücher zur versandkostenfreien Lieferung innerhalb Deutschlands an folgende Anschrift:

Vorname, Name: _____

Straße, Hausnr.: _____

PLZ, Ort: _____

Tel. (für Rückfragen): _____ *Datum, Unterschrift:* _____

Zahlungsart

❐ *ich möchte per Rechnung zahlen*

❐ *ich möchte per Lastschrift zahlen*

bei Zahlung per Lastschrift bitte ausfüllen:

Kontoinhaber: _____

Kreditinstitut: _____

Kontonummer: _____ Bankleitzahl: _____

Hiermit ermächtige ich jederzeit widerruflich den *ibidem*-Verlag, die fälligen Zahlungen für mein Abonnement der **Schriftenreihe Masterstudiengang Consumer Health Care** von meinem oben genannten Konto per Lastschrift abzubuchen.

Datum, Unterschrift: _____

Abonnementformular entweder **per Fax** senden an: **0511 / 262 2201** oder 0711 / 800 1889
oder als **Brief** an: *ibidem*-Verlag, Julius-Leber Weg 11, 30457 Hannover oder
als e-mail an: ibidem@ibidem-verlag.de

ibidem-Verlag
Melchiorstr. 15
D-70439 Stuttgart
info@ibidem-verlag.de

www.ibidem-verlag.de
www.ibidem.eu
www.edition-noema.de
www.autorenbetreuung.de

Zeitfracht Medien GmbH
Ferdinand-Jühlke-Straße 7
99095 Erfurt, Deutschland
produktsicherheit@kolibri360.de